Southern Black Creative Writers, 1829–1953

Biobibliographies

Compiled by
M. Marie Booth Foster

Bibliographies and Indexes in Afro-American
and African Studies, Number 22

GREENWOOD PRESS
New York • Westport, Connecticut • London

Library of Congress Cataloging-in-Publication Data

Foster, M. Marie Booth.
  Southern Black creative writers, 1829-1953 : biobibliographies /
compiled by M. Marie Booth Foster.
    p. cm. – (Bibliographies and indexes in Afro-American and
African studies, ISSN 0742-6925 ; no. 22)
  Bibliography: p.
  Includes index.
  ISBN 0-313-26207-1 (lib. bdg. : alk. paper)
  1. American literature – Afro-American authors – Bio-bibliography.
2. American literature – Southern States – Bio-bibliography. 3. Afro-
American authors – Southern States – Biography – Dictionaries.
I. Title. II. Series.
Z1229.N39F67 1988
[PS153.N5]
016.81 '09 '896073 – dc19   88-5595

British Library Cataloguing in Publication Data is available.

Library of Congress Catalog Card Number: 88-5595
ISBN: 0-313-26207-1
ISSN: 0742-6925

First published in 1988

Greenwood Press, Inc.
88 Post Road West, Westport, Connecticut 06881

∞

The paper used in this book complies with the
Permanent Paper Standard issued by the National
Information Standards Organization (Z39.48-1984).

10 9 8 7 6 5 4 3 2 1

Contents

Acknowledgments   vii

Introduction   ix

Explanation of Biobibliographical Notes   xvi

Southern Black Writers and Their Works, 1829-1953   1

Appendixes   73
     Author Listing By State   73
     Author Listing By Period   78

Selected Bibliography of Southern Black Writers,
    1829-1953   84

References   103

Acknowledgments

Along my way, during the past few years, I have had the good fortune to correspond or work with librarians for many of the major repositories of black literature. To them I offer my gratitude, especially the librarians at Atlanta University Center and Florida A&M University libraries. I am deeply indebted to the Florida A&M University Research Committee for the grant that enabled me to do a great deal of the research for this book.

    I would like to give special thanks to my children, Kendra and Charles, and their father, Charles Andrew, who probably wondered when the experience would end; and to my parents, Lemuel and Etta Booth, and my grandmother, Mamie Booth, for their inspiration.

Introduction

William Pickens recounts in *The Vengeance of the Gods and Three Other Stories of Color Line Life* (1922) the story of a little boy who asks his mother why lions are always shown to be frightening to people and easily whipped. His mother explains to him, "My Son, it's like this; those lions did not paint the picture." This perhaps, is a clue to the early purposes of Southern black writers: they did not want to suffer the fate of the lion.

Although many of the early depictions did not reach a wide audience because they were privately printed by the author or simply not considered as worthy of note, Southern black writers have shown themselves fully capable of "painting pictures" of themselves and the gaiety and sadness of their existence. For this reason alone, it is important that they be identified and reviewed as important "marks" in Southern literary history. That they commanded a seemingly minor audience, that their early writing styles have been described as unrefined, in comparison to their white counterparts, should be of little importance.

The number of writers who put pen and ink to paper from 1829-1953 was far greater than it is possible for this bibliography to reflect. A search of the literature of towns and hamlets in the remote areas will quite possibly yield a community poet, dramatist, or writer of fiction who was known only to that community.

College campuses were also definite fertile grounds for writers. In the late 1800s when normal schools for blacks began operation, shortages of teachers and funds were major problems. Because active minds will be creative and because of the necessity for creativity, many teachers--regardless of their areas of expertise--were called upon to offer instruction for extracurricular activities. Some found it necessary to become creative writers, writing original material for performances--material to supplement the classics. Therefore, a notable number of Southern black writers were normal school and college teachers--some of whom were also ministers, who began writing out of necessity and continued because of desire.

Of those who sought their "promised land" in the North, there were some brilliant though uneducated minds that produced literature, sometimes with the help of federal work projects, but often on their own while working at another occupation.

And then there were those who were privately printed authors. Because of their blackness, many, if not most, of the early black writers found this the only avenue available to them to publish their work. White benefactors were not always waiting in line to help the struggling black writer. In a number of cases, the A.M.E. and Baptist churches opened their presses to authors, printing and reprinting selected creative writing for the benefit of their members.

In order to understand the plight of Southern black writers and the obstacles they encountered, it is helpful to review a bit of black American history from 1829 to 1953. For this discussion, this 124-year period will be divided into four sections: From Slavery to Freedom, 1829-1865; Reconstruction to 1912; From Migration to Depression, 1913-1928; and Oppressed, Depressed, Suppressed, but Determined, 1929-1953.

From Slavery to Freedom, 1829-1865

During the years 1829-1865, Southern black writers were confronted with the major complication in the lives of the black people in the South: slavery. In most cases, the incentive to write fiction, poetry, and drama was provided by this complication and the need to combat it as well as to make nonblacks and blacks understand its wrongs. Perhaps writing fulfilled the need for intellectual exercise more intense and more logical than the emotion-filled spirituals, and less fictional and more factual than the animal-imageried folktales of traditional black culture. However, even with the problems of slavery ever present, Southern black writers found time to see some, though not many, positive aspects of the South, such as its physical beauty, and to present their feelings about their love, laughter, and their God.

New perspectives of the South were introduced into Southern literature when George Moses Horton's *Hope of Liberty* was published in 1829, followed by the novels, plays, short stories, and poetry of Frances

Watkins Harper, Harriet Wilson--though her identity as a Southern writer is questioned by researchers, William Wells Brown, and Martin Delaney. Earlier, while white writers were writing of their South, a South they quite often saw through rose-colored glasses, Southern blacks were making their views known in their oral literature, which included folktales and the lyrics of spirituals. Beginning with Horton, however, they began to publish their views of the South--its people, their ideologies, and mostly their desire for freedom.

Slavery, that peculiar institution that was rationalized as having been sanctioned by the Bible, created an attitude of uncertainty in the South, giving black writers much to react to through their literature. The writers saw laws being passed to further limit the rights of blacks and to curtail the work of abolitionists and to expand the institution. They experienced slave auctions, slavehunts, lynchings, inhumane treatment of slaves on the plantation, owners living in luxury while slaves lived in extreme poverty, moral abuse of slaves, the anger of the poor whites, and comradeship with the Indians and white abolitionists. Writers had to defeat the romantic portraitures of plantation literature, which exaggerated many of the superficially attractive features of the South and plantation life, while simultaneously overlooking the ugliness of slavery. Plantation literature was in many ways a forensic tool reflecting the South's fear of the abolitionists, slave insurrections, and the loss of needed slave labor for increasing agricultural opportunity.

The black writers during this period did not astound the world with their talent and penchant for writing, but they changed the face of Southern literature by adding a few black touches. They, like their counterparts, sometimes fell short of a realistic portrait of the South in their pleas and arguments for black freedom. The group, however, did consist of some notable firsts in publication history: the first black woman novelist, Harriet Wilson; the first black playwright, William Wells Brown; and the first black woman short fiction writer, Frances Watkins Harper.

Reconstruction to 1912

Though the cloud by day, fire by night atmosphere of the South dominated the thoughts of blacks during

Reconstruction, other subjects were factors in black writers' creativity, making their writings more than mere appraisals of the South. Still the separation of the art of writing from propaganda about conditions in the South was not evident, even though writers, many of whom were former slaves, were becoming more and more products of the black middle class, attempting to create for a white audience that was still overlooking their existence.

Reconstruction was a period of chaos, a period when most blacks thought that freedom was going to solve all of their problems and reward them with acknowledgment of their manhood and womanhood. They thought that their rights would be gained instantaneously. Others knew from firsthand experience that the downtrodden South would not hand them freedom on a silver platter. They learned a great deal about the overrated item, paper. The laws on paper were not the laws that had been filed in the mentality of the Southern white and, quite often, the Southern black. While property, they were protected because they were valuable; as citizens, they were nuisances and a source of embarrassment to a South that had lost most of its prosperity and a good deal of its esteem.

Blacks did not allow the threats of violence to deter them from their course. With the help of some Northerners and a few virtuous Southerners, they sought education, property, and a voice in politics. But they witnessed not only discrimination and segregation but an increase in the number of lynchings and the curtailing of education around the 1890s. Some historians refer to the 1870s through the early 1900s as the darkest period--a period when the rights gained as a result of the Civil War were taken away.

The majority of the writers publishing during this period wrote of some Southern element, although the choice was not always to focus on the present. Sometimes the choice was simply to write about the flowers, trees, birds, old mansions, and the landscape.

Writers during this period include Francis Boyd, Albery A. Whitman, John Willis Menard, William Wells Brown, J. McHenry Jones, Francis Watkins Harper, Daniel Webster Davis, James Weldon Johnson, Timothy Fortune, Charles W. Chesnutt, and Sutton Griggs. The writings ranged from dialect tongue-twisting to melodrama. Publishers did not rush to publish them, and as a result many works were privately printed.

Charles Chesnutt found that his identity as a black writer had to be shielded from the reading audience to ensure sales. In an effort to write to sell, he created conjure stories/folktales. Many of the writers in this group helped to set the stage for the Negro Renaissance of the 1920s.

From Migration to Depression, 1913-1928

During the years 1913 to 1928, the most notable occurrences in the South were migration, lynching, riots, and the making of the film, *Birth of a Nation*, and the resulting revival of the KKK. Though blacks migrated from the South to the North after the Civil War and before 1913, migration beginning in 1913 was like a tidal wave. Increased anxiety about getting ahead and the failure of the cotton crops, not to mention the highly publicized employment opportunities in the North, influenced many to go North. Though they were often frustrated by the conditions found while living in the vast ghettoes of the North, they still seemed to prefer life in the North to life in the South.

Between 1921 and 1924, migration was spurred on both by the discontent of the black soldiers who never experienced the honor or esteem granted the white soldiers, and the loss of jobs to whites. Various movements took place to organize the black farmers, but seemingly to no avail. A great distinction was made between "black work" and "white work" after 1910, and as a result, blacks found only menial jobs, if any at all. Most of the jobs available in expanding areas went to whites. Unions would either limit the number of black tradesmen they accepted or accept none at all. The International Longshoremen's Association organized in the 1890s was one of the few unions that accepted blacks.

Negro soldiers endangered their own and their families' lives when they returned South after participating in World War I. Some soldiers could not forget the treatment they received overseas; they had been treated as equal to white men. Lynching served to remind them that they were not. Lynching supposedly declined just before World War I, but tensions rose at the end of the war and the savagery again became a trend. There was another decline in lynching from 1919 to 1924, but the toll rose once more at the outset of the Depression.

The KKK experienced a revival with the release of the movie, *Birth of a Nation*. The film gave new impetus to the KKK, the self-proclaimed saviours of white women and civilization in the South.

What was begrudgingly given the black man after the Civil War, the white South schemingly attempted to retract, and quite often did. Before 1913, reduced voting by blacks was caused by legal restrictions, taxes, and literacy requirements, but in 1924, it was violence that prevented blacks from exercising their rights at the polls.

Writers at this time who chose to write about the South that existed between 1913 and 1928 dealt with all of the factors and concerns in their writing. Those who chose to write about the past, still chose to present a troubled South. Writers during this era included F. Gilmore Sims, Otis Shackleford, James Weldon Johnson, Leslie Pinckney Hill, William Pickens, Jean Toomer, Joshua H. Jones, and Walter White. Many of the writers could write from firsthand experience because of their choice to be a part of the NAACP and other like groups. The outlet for publishing at this point included a number of black-edited/owned journals, newspapers, and magazines.

Oppressed, Depressed, Suppressed, but Determined, 1829–1953

When the Great Depression began in 1929, the South had already experienced agricultural crises as well as those in business and industry. Riots and other incidents made the Southerners leery of labor unions and strikers, which they considered precursors to communism and attempts at social equality for the black man. The KKK was not a grand participant, but believers in white supremacy banded together against the labor unions, the strikers, and the overzealous black man.

The New Deal brought hope for some people, but in many cases blacks in the South reaped few of the rewards. Government programs, such as the Agricultural Adjustment Administration, were instituted, but blacks had little voice in the administration of the programs and thus received little benefit. They saw themselves as no better off when more and more progress was supposedly being made. Almost everything was segregated and unequal.

The voice of the black man became louder and louder as the years passed. And as the voice of the black man in general became louder, black writers had more time to devote to subjects other than those directly connected with their plight as black men and women. The number of those being published also increased during this time. Blacks banded together to fight discrimination, the continued violence directed at them, the segregation that occurred even in the armed forces as the United States became involved in World War II, Jim Crow laws that would not allow blacks fair treatment, the double standards of the courtroom, and anything else that affected the progress of the black man in the South and in America. Blacks would make much headway in 1954 with the Supreme Court decision in the case *Brown vs. the Board of Education*.

Writers during this period included Willis Richardson, Sterling Brown, Richard Wright, John H. Hill, Randolph Edmonds, Arna Bontemps, George W. Lee, and Frank Yerby, all of whom demonstrated advancement in artistry, dealing with such varied topics as the family to love relationships to politics. Black writers began to exploit not only the topics related to their social well-being, but those related to views of self, family, friends--subjects they did not choose to write about when they were writing to be read by a white audience.

Together, the Southern black writers that published between 1829 and 1953 wrote about practically every subject: economics, education, society, religion, laws, the press, family, politics. They expressed views that were both realistic and romanticized or melodramatic, as they explored seriously and comically the mysterious and fascinating pain and beauty of the South. When reviewing the list of Southern black writers, it becomes obvious that the South was a foundry of creativity. The many irons inserted into that foundry, after becoming heated and molded, gave many others ideas about how to mold their own irons. Thoughts, styles and conventions in the literature of writers from other areas indicate that the South and its Southern writers are a great part of the legacy of black writing in the United States.

Explanation of Biobibliographical Notes

This biobibliography was written in an attempt to identify for posterity as many Southern black writers as possible who were writing between 1829-1953, and whose legacy as writers should not be underestimated. The term "Southern" is used in this work as a descriptor of those writers who were born or spent time in the former Confederate States of America, and Maryland, Washington, D.C., Kentucky, and West Virginia. Many of the writers previously have not been considered significant enough to appear in the widely circulated literary biographies/dictionaries. At first, I sought to identify only those writers who had published volumes. Realizing that to do this was to exclude a part of the legacy, I used research gathered from periodicals, including *The Messenger*, *Opportunity*, *The Crisis*, *Carolina*, *Fire*, *and Negro History Bulletin*, and anthologies to identify those writers whose poetry, short fiction, and drama frequently appeared in periodicals and anthologies, and who may never have compiled a volume, or if so, did not do so until after 1953.

A variety of sources were used to provide a bibliographical listing of creative works by the authors identified. (See Appendixes for references used.) A selected bibliography of each author's works that do not fit the category "creative writing"--fiction, poetry, or drama--is also given.

The biographical information for some of the writers will appear somewhat sketchy, but it is felt that even a sketch identifying the writer as *Southern*, *black*, and *a writer*, is better than no information at all. Since many of the writers wrote as a second vocation or even as a hobby, it was quite difficult to find biographical details about some of them. At all times, attention was given to such details as date of birth and death, schooling and occupation, honors and awards received, and of course, their literary works. Some of the references given in the appendixes will provide other details about some of the writers, but about others little is known, available, or accessible.

Format of Notes

Name of Writer (date of birth - date of death, birthplace or place of residence while in the South) vocation/occupation, identification by genre written

Bibliography of Creative Writings

(Listing of where creative writings appeared, such as periodicals or anthologies)

Biographical Information--education, work experiences, honors, awards, nonfiction, writings after 1953

[*References by number*--bibliography of references will be numbered.]

.

Southern Black Creative Writers, 1829–1953

Southern Black Writers
and Their Works,
1829–1953

Alba, Nanina (1915-1968, Montgomery, AL) teacher, poet

  (In *The Poetry of the Negro*, 1949; *Phylon*, *Negro Digest*, *Peninsula Poets*, *Message Magazine*)

Attended Haines Institute, Augusta, Georgia; Knoxville College (B.A., 1935); and Indiana University. Taught English, French, and music at Tuskegee Institute. Published *The Parchments*, 1963 and *The Parchments II*, 1967.
[1, 31, 42]

Albert, Octavia V. Rogers (1853-1890, Oglethorpe, GA) slave, teacher, author

  The House of Bondage, or Charlotte Brooks and Other Slaves. New York: Hunt and Eaton, 1890.
  (pictorial essay-slave narratives)

Attended Atlanta University, receiving training as teacher. Participant in numerous activities of the Methodist Church; taught in Georgia.
[36]

Alexander, Lewis (1900-1945, educated in Washington, D.C. schools) actor, editor, poet

  (In *The Carolina Magazine*--1930, *The Crisis*--1923, *Opportunity*, and J.C. Byars's *Black and White* (1927) and other anthologies)

Attended Howard University and the University of Pennsylvania. Associated with the Ethiopian Art Theatre Company, the Playwriters Circle, and the Ira Aldridge Players. Directed the Randall Community Center players and the Ira Aldridge Players of the Grover Cleveland Centre. Specialized in haiku poetry.
[13, 39]

Alexander, Truman Hudson (1891- , AL) novelist

  Loot. 1932. rpt. Freeport, NY: Books for Libraries Press,1972.
[55]

Allen, George Leonard (1905-1935, Lumberton, NC) teacher, poet

(In *Opportunity, American Life, The Southwestern Christian Advocate,* and *The Lyric West,* the *Church School Journal,* and in *Caroling Dusk* and other anthologies)

Attended Redstone Academy in Lumberton, North Carolina and Johnson C. Smith (B.S., 1926). Teaching assignments included Kendall Institute in Sumter, South Carolina. Won first prize for poem, "To Melody," in a statewide poetry contest sponsored by the North Carolina United Daughters of the Confederacy.
[17, 34]

Allen, Junius Mordecai (1875-1906, Montgomery, AL) poet, boilermaker, and theatrical performer

Rhymes, Tales and Rhymed Tales. Topeka, KS: Crane & Co., 1906.

Family moved to Topeka, Kansas when he was 7. Attended public school in Topeka. Boiler maker at 17, leaving the profession to travel with a theatrical company. Returned to boilermaking when the company folded.
[56]

Andrews, W.T. (pastored in Talladega, AL) novelist

A Waif--a Prince; or, A Mother's Triumph. Freeport, New York: Books for Libraries Press, 1972.

Minister in the North Alabama Conference, M.E. Church.
[Preface to novel]

Arneaux, J.A. (1855- , GA) tragedian, editor, poet

(In anthologies and magazines)

Early schooling at Beech Institute and then in the North. Worked as writer on the staff of the *New York World* and the *New York Sun.* Referred to as the "Black Booth."
[53]

Ashby, William M. (1889- , James City, VA) novelist

  Redder Blood. New York: Cosmopolitan, 1915.
  The Road to Damascus. Boston: Christopher, 1935.

Executive Secretary of the New Jersey Urban League in
the 1920s.

Attaway, William Alexander (1911- , Greenville, MS)
salesman, labor organizer, playwright, novelist

  Let Me Breathe Thunder. New York: Doubleday and
  Doran, 1939.
  Blood on the Forge. New York: Doubleday,
  1941.

His father took the family North during the Great
Migration. Schooled in the Chicago school system and
at the University of Illinois (B.A.). Wrote plays:
Carnival (produced in 1945), *The Tale of the Black
Moor* (published in *Challenger*, June 1936). Acted in
You Can't Take It With You--his sister got him the
part.   Other published works include *The Calypso Song
Book* (1957) and *Hear America Singing* (1967). Awarded
the Rosenwald Fellowship to work on his second novel.
Wrote scripts for television and arranged songs for
Harry Belafonte.
[35]

Ayers, Vivian (Chester, SC) teacher, poet, playwright

  Spice Dawns. New York: Exposition, 1953.
  Bow Boly, a play.

Attended Barbara-Scotia in Concordia; graduated from
Bennett College in Greensboro (B.S.). Taught at the
University of Houston.
[29]

Banks, William Augustus (TN) poet

  Gathering Dusk. Chattanooga, TN: The Wilson
  Printing Co., 1935.
  Lest We Forget. Chattanooga, TN: Central High
  Press, 1930.
  Beyond the Rockies and Other Poems. Philadephia:
  Doran & Co., 1926.

Barber, J. Max (1878- , Blackstock, SC) editor, poet

(In *Opportunity*)

Graduated from Virginia Union University, Richmond, and a dental school in Philadephia, Pennsylvania. Edited *Voice of the Negro*; listed as contributing editor to several issues of *Crisis*.
[*33*]

Battle, Effie Dean Threat (Okolona, MS ?) poet

   Gleanings from Dixieland. Tuskegee Institute, AL:
     Tuskegee Institute, 1914.

Wife of Wallace Battle who was born in Alabama. Worked in Mississippi.
[*57*]

Beadle, Samuel Alfred (1857-1932, Atlanta, GA) lawyer, poet

   Sketches from Life in Dixie. Chicago: Scroll
     Publishing and Literary Syndicate, 1899.
   Adam Shuffler. Jackson, MS: Harmon Publishing
     Co., 1901.
   Lyrics of the Underworld. Jackson, MS: W.A. Scott,
     1912.

Studied law in Mississippi. Practiced law in Mississippi.
[*35, 52*]

Benjamin, Robert C.O. (1855- , schooled and worked in the South) attorney, lecturer, journalist, educator, and poet

   Poetic Gems. Charlotteville, VA: Peck and Allen
     Printers, 1883.
   The Defender of Obadiah Cuff. (n.d.)

Attended Trinity College in Oxford, Virginia. Studied law with Kentucky State Attorney Dave Smith and with Josiah Patterson of Memphis, Tennessee. Worked as a soliciting agent for *New York Star*, city editor of the *Progressive American*, letter carrier in New York Post Office for helping in Rutherford B. Hayes'campaign, school teacher in Kentucky and Arkansas, principal of high school in Decatur, Alabama, editor of the *Negro American* in Birmingham, Alabama. Owned and edited the *Colored Citizen* in Pittsburgh and the *Chronicle* in Evansville, Indiana.
[*52, 53*]

Bibb, Eloise Thompson (-1928, New Orleans, LA)
social worker, feature writer, dramatist

   Poems. 1895. rpt. Freeport, New York: Books for
     Libraries Press, 1971.
   (Produced plays: *Africannus*. Los Angeles, 1922;
   Caught. The Ethiopian Folk Players, 1925; *Cooped Up*,
   New York, 1925.)

Received early schooling in New Orleans, studied at
Oberlin College and Howard University, and New York
School of Philanthrophy. Head Resident of the Social
Settlement House of Howard University, Washington,
D.C.   Special feature writer for Sunday issue of the
Los Angeles Tribune, and *The Morning Sun of Los
Angeles*.
[50]

Bohanan, Otto Leland (Washington, D.C.) musician,
poet

   (In *Opportunity*, 1920s)

Graduated from Howard University.   Taught in St.
Louis and New York.
[16]

Bond, Frederick W. (Windsor, NC) teacher, author,
playwright, poet

   Family Affair; a one act play. [Institute]: West
     Virginia State College, 1939.

Attended secondary schools in Washington, D.C. and
North Carolina; graduated from Howard (B.S., 1927),
Columbia (M.A., 1930), and New York University
(Ph.D., 1938). Taught at Johnson C. Smith (1930-
1937), West Virginia State (1938-1940), and Stowe
Teachers College--Missouri (1940-). Nonfiction works
include: a textbook, *Speech Construction* (1936), and
The Negro and the Drama (1940). Wrote at least six
plays.
[51]

Bonner, Marita (1905- , born in MA, but worked in
Washington, D.C.) teacher,

essays, plays and short stories, published in
Crisis and *Opportunity*)

Attended school in Massachusetts (B.A., Radcliffe
College). Taught English in Washington, D.C. school
system. Awarded *Opportunity* literary award for short
story, "Tin Can," in 1934.
[25]

Bontemps, Arna Wendell (1902-1973, Alexandria, LA)
teacher, librarian, poet, novelist

> *God Sends Sunday.* New York: Harcourt, Brace and
>   Co., 1931.
> (With Langston Hughes) *Popo and Fifina, Children of
>   Haiti.* New York: Macmillan Co., 1932.
> *You Can't Pet a Possum.* New York: W. Morrow and
>   Co., 1934.
> *Black Thunder.* 1936. rpt. Boston: Beacon Press,
>   1968.
> *Sad-Faced Boy.* Boston: Houghton Mifflin, 1937.
> *Drums at Dusk.* New York: Macmillan, 1939.
> (With Jack Conroy) *The Fast Sooner Hound*, 1942.
> (With Jack Conroy) *Slappy Hooper, The Wonderful
>   Sign Painter.* Boston: Houghton Mifflin, 1946.
> (With Langston Hughes) *St. Louis Woman*, 1946.
> *Sam Patch, the High Wide and Handsome Jumper.* 1951.

Attended elementary school in California, Pacific
Union College (B.S., 1923), the University of Chicago
(Rosenwald Scholarship--M.A. in Library Science,
1942), and Columbia University. Taught in New York
(private schools, 1923-1931); Oakwood Junior College-
Huntsville, Alabama (1931-1934); Shiloh Academy-
Chicago (1935-1938); chief librarian and professor of
creative writing at Fisk (1943-1965) and worked in
the University's public relations office (1965-).
Awards and honors included Julius Rosenwald
Fellowship (1938-1939, 1942-1943), Guggenheim
Fellowship, *Opportunity*'s Alexander Pushkin Award for
"Golgotha Is a Mountain" (1926), and the same award
for "The Return" (1927), first prize in the 1927
Crisis-sponsored poetry contest for "Nocturne at
Bethesda," Jane Addams Children's Book Award for
Story of the Negro (1956), and the James I. Dow Award
of the Society of Midland Authors for *Anyplace But
Here* (written with Jack Conroy) in 1967. Books of
nonfiction for children include *Fredrick Douglass*
(1959) and *100 Years of Freedom* (1961). Published
also for children, *Lonesome Boy* (1955). Edited works

include *Golden Slippers* (1941), *American Negro Poetry*
(1963), and with Langston Hughes, *The Poetry of the
Negro* (1949, 1970). Also, edited the autobiography of
W.C. Handy, *The Father of the Blues*. Articles in
The Horn Book, *Common Ground*, *Opportunity*, *Survey
Graphic*. Reviews in *Herald Tribune Books* and the
Chicago Bookweek.
[2, 36, 42]

Borders, William Holmes (1905- , Swift Creek, near
Macon, GA) minister, poet

  Thunderbolts (poems). Atlanta: Morris Brown
   College Press, 1942.

Attended Morehouse. Received honorary degrees from
Atlanta University and Howard University (1966).
Civic leader--led his church in sponsorship of
housing project. Pastored in Georgia.
[57]

Boyd, Francis A. (1844-1872, KY) minister, poet

  Columbiana; or the North Star. Chicago: Steam and
   Job Printing House of B. Hand, 1870.

Chaplain in Union Army.
[4, 46, 52]

Braithwaite, William Stanley Beaumont (1878-1962,
worked in the South) professor, anthologist, critic,
poet

  The Canadian. Boston: Small, Maynard and Co.,
   1901.
  Lyrics of Life and Love. Boston: H.B. Turner and
   Co., 1904.
  The House of Falling Leaves with Other Poems.
   Boston: J.W. Luce and Co., 1908.
  Going Over Tindel. Boston: B.J. Brimmer Co., 1924.
  Selected Poems. New York: Coward-McCann, Inc.,
   1948.

Self-educated--left school at thirteen to help
family. Taught at Atlanta University (1935-1945); was
a compositor for Ginn and Company, on editorial staff
for the *Boston Transcript*. Edited numerous poetry
anthologies: *The Book of Elizabethan Verse* (1906),
The Book of Georgian Verse (1908), *The Book of*

Restoration Verse (1909), *Anthology of Magazine Verse
and Year Book of American Poetry*--seventeen volumes
(1913-1929), *Golden Treasury of Magazine Verse*
(1918), *The Book of Modern British Verse* (1919),
Victory (1919), *Anthology of Massachusetts* (1922),
*Our Lady's Choir, A Contemporary Anthology of Verse
by Catholic Sisters* (1931). Authored *The Poetic Year
for 1916, The Story of the Great War* (1919), *Our
Essays and Critics of Today* (1920), *A Fragment
Wrenched from the Life of Titus Jabson* (1928), *The
House Under Arcturus; An Autobiography* (1941).
Received awards and honors such as the Spingharn
Medal for outstanding achievement by an American
Negro (1918), honorary M.A. from Atlanta University
(1918), and an honorary Litt.D. from Talladega
College (1918). Articles, critical essays, and
occasional poems appeared in magazines and journals,
including *The New Republic, Journal of Education,
North American Review, Atlantic Monthly, Scribner's*
and *Phylon*.
[36]

Brawley, Benjamin (1882-1939, Columbia, SC)
professor, minister, dean, editor, poet

  A Prayer. Atlanta: Atlanta Baptist College Press,
   1899.
  A Toast to Love and Death. Atlanta: Atlanta
   Baptist College Print, 1902.
  The Problem and Other Poems. Atlanta: Author,
   1905.
  The Desire of the Moth for the Star. Atlanta: The
   Franklin-Turner Co., 1906.
  The Dawn and Other Poems. Washington, D.C.:
   Author, 1911.
  The Seven Sleepers of Ephesus. (lyrical legend)
   Atlanta: Foster and Davies, 1917.

Educated at Atlanta Baptist College, renamed
Morehouse (B.A., 1901), the University of Chicago
(A.B., 1907) and Harvard (M.A., 1908). Worked at
Morehouse (1902-1910, 1912-1920), Shaw (1923-1931),
and Howard (1911, 1931-1939). Wrote a number of non-
fiction works, including *A Short History of the
American Negro* (1913), *History of Morehouse* (1917),
The Negro in Literature and Art (1918)--revised to
The Negro Genius (1937), *A Social History of the
American Negro* (1921; 1971), *A Short History of
American Drama* (1921), *A New Survey of English
Literature* (1925), *Freshman Year English* (1929),

Doctor Dillard of the Jeanes Fund (1930), *A History of the English Hymn* (1932), *Paul Laurence Dunbar: Poet of His People* (1936), *Negro Builders and Heroes* (1937) and numerous articles and reviews in *The Dial, Dictionary of American Biography, Lipponcott's Magazine*, the *Springfield Republican, The Bookman, Sewanee Review, Southern Workman, North American Review*, and the *Harvard Monthly*. Declined Harmon Foundation's second place award for excellence in education, 1927.
[36]

Brooks, Jonathan Henderson (1904-1945, near Lexington, MS) educator, minister, poet

   The Resurrection and Other Poems. Dallas:
   Kaleidoscope Press, 1948.

Attended grade school at Jackson College in Mississippi, Lincoln University in Missouri, and college at Tougaloo College. Taught in Mississippi. Contributed to *Opportunity*.
[17]

Brooks, Rosa Paul (Nashville, TN) poet

   Poetic Meditations. 1945.
[24]

Brooks, Walter Henderson (1851-1945, Richmond, VA) minister, poet

   Original Poems. Washington, D.C.: The Sunday
   School of the Church in connection with his 50th
   anniversary as pastor, 1932.
   The Pastor's Voice, a Collection of Poems.
   Washington, D.C.: Associated, 1945.

Educated at preparatory school of Lincoln University (Pennsylvania), Lincoln University (B.A., 1872; B.D., 1873, LL.D., 1929), and Howard University (D.D., 1944). Served as Sunday School Missionary for the American Baptist Publication Society (1874-1876, 1880-1882), pastor of the Second African Baptist Church--Richmond, Virginia (1877-1880), Pastor of the 19th street Baptist Church in Washington, D.C.(1880-1945); Chaplain of the Anti-Saloon League.
[36, 52]

Brown, Charlotte Hawkins (1882-1961, Henderson, NC) educator, writer

"Mammy," a *Story of Negro Fidelity and Southern Neglect.* Pilgrim Press, 1919.

Attended the Massachusetts State Normal School at Salem (1901), Harvard Summer School (1901, 1909), and Simmons College (1917). Received honorary degrees from Livingstone College and North Carolina College (A.M., 1921), Wilberforce University (LL.D., 1932), Lincoln University-Oxford, Pennsylvania (LL.D., 1937), and Howard University (Ed.D., 1944); educator at and founder of the Palmer Memorial Institute.
[36, 57]

Brown, Handy Nereus. (AL) musician, composer, writer

  The Necromancer. 1904. rpt. New York: AMS Press, 1970.
[57]

Brown, Sterling (1901- , Washington, D.C.) author, professor, poet

  Southern Road. New York: Harcourt, Brace and Co., 1932.

Educated at Williams (B.S.) and Harvard (M.A.); received the Guggenheim Fellowship for creative writing in 1937 (*Southern Road*). Served as advisor on Negro Studies for the Federal Writers Project, 1938-1939. Worked at Howard University, Virginia Seminary and College, Fisk University, Lincoln University, New York University, Sarah Lawrence, Vassar, and the New School (New York). Nonfiction: *Negro in American Fiction* (1937), *Negro Poetry and Drama* (1937), co-author of *Negro Caravan; Writings by American Negroes* (1941). Contributed articles and poems to *Opportunity*, *Survey Graphic* and other magazines and journals, and to anthologies. Retired from Howard University in 1969, but still teaches literature courses. Received honorary degrees from the University of Massachusetts, Howard University, and Northwestern University. Published *The Last Ride of Will Bill* in 1974.
[22]

Brown, William Wells (1814-1884, Lexington, KY) abolitionist, novelist, dramatist

  The Anti-Slavery Harp: a collection of songs for anti-slavery meetings. Boston: B.J. Marsh, 1848.

*Clotel; or the President's Daughter: A Narrative
of Slave Life in the United States.* 1853. rpt. New
York: Arno Press, 1969.
*Experience; Or, How to Give a Northern Man a
Backbone.* 1856.
*The Escape; or A Leap for Freedom, a drama in five
acts.* Boston: R.F. Walcut, 1858.
*Miralda; or, the Beautiful Quadroon. A Romance of
Slavery.* Founded in Fact, 1860-1861. Published in
Weekly Anglo-African, Nov. 30-March 16.
Clotelle: A Tale of the Southern States, 1864.
Boston: James Redpath, 1955.
*Clotelle; or, the Colored Heroine. A Tale of
Southern States.* 1867. rpt. Miami: Mnemosyne
Publishing, Inc., 1969.

Born a slave. Self-educated; studied medicine
privately and as an apprentice. Practiced medicine,
but devoted much of his time to lecturing and
writing. Served as lecturing agent for the Western
New York Anti-Slavery Society (1843-1847), and the
Massachusetts and the American Anti-Slavery Societies
(1847-1849); lecturer in Great Britain (1849-1854).
Wrote more than a dozen books and pamphlets,
including *Narrative of William W. Brown, a Fugitive
Slave, Written By Himself* (1847), *Three Years in
Europe; or, Places I Have Seen and People I Have Met*
(1852), *The American Fugitive in Europe; Sketches of
Places and People Abroad* (1855), *St. Domingo: Its
Revolutions and Its Patriots* (1855), *The Black Man,
His Antecedents, His Genius, and His Achievements*
(1863 et seq.), *The Negro in the American
Rebellion: His Heroism and His Fidelity* (1867), *The
Rising Son; Or, The Antecedents and Advancement of
the Colored Race* (1874), *My Southern Home; Or, The
South and Its People* (1880).
[36]

Brownlee, Julius Pinkney (1886- , South Carolina)
poet

  Ripples. Anderson, SC: Cox Stationery Co.,
  1914.

Bruce, John Edward "Bruce Grit" (1856-1924,
Piscataway, MD) journalist, historian, novelist

  The Awakening of Hezekiah Jones. Hopkinsville, KY:
  Phil H. Brown, 1916.

Born a slave. Basically self-educated--attended
public school in Stratford, Connecticut, public and
private instruction in Washington, D.C. with some
study at Howard University. Helped Schomberg and
others to organize the Negro Society for Historical
Research in 1911. Founded the *Argus*, a weekly
newspaper in Washington, D.C. (1879), the *Sunday Item*
(1880), the *Washington Grit* (1884), with Charles
Anderson--the *Chronicle of New York City* (1897), and
the *Weekly Standard of Yonkers* (1908). Worked for
more than twenty black newspapers and wrote articles
that appeared in some white papers. Worked for the
Port of New York Authority most of his adult life.
Nonfiction publications include a book, *Short
Biographical Sketches of Eminent Negro Men and Women
in Europe and the United States* (1910); pamphlets,
The Blot of the Escutcheon, *Concentration of Energy*,
The Blood Red Record, *The Making of a Race*, *a Tribute
to the Negro Soldier*, and *Tracts for the People*.
"Bruce Grit" was his famous column head in the
Gazette of Cleveland and the *New York Age*.
[36]

Bruce, Richard--Richard Bruce Nugent (1905-,
Washington, D.C.) specialist in art and drama,
dramatist

  (In *The New Negro*, 1925, and *Plays and Pageants*,
  1930, and in *Fire*, 1926)

Attended public school in Washington, D.C.
[33]

Burroughs, Margaret G. (1917- , St. Rose, LA)
artist, teacher, museum director, juvenile writer

  Jasper the Drummin' Boy. New York: Viking, 1947.
  (children's story)

Attended Chicago Normal College (Elementary Teachers
Certificate, 1937; Upper Grade Art Certificate,
1939), Art Institute of Chicago (B.A., art education,
1946; M.A., art education, 1948), Esmerelda Art
School in Mexico City (1953), Columbia University
Teachers College (postgraduate work, summers, 1958-
1960). School teacher in Chicago; founder, Director
of the Museum of African-American history, 1961- ;
professor at Chicago Art Institute and Kennedy-King
College.
[42]

Butcher, James W., Jr. (1909- , Washington, D.C.)
playwright

  The Seer. In *Negro Caravan*. 1941.
  Milk and Honey

Attended public school in Washington, D.C. and
college at Howard University, the University of
Illinois (A.B., 1932), and the University of Iowa
(M.A., 1941). Taught at Atlanta University, Summer
School of Theatre. Helped to organize and direct the
Negro Repertory Theatre of Washington, and served as
director of the Howard University Players.
[11]

Butler, Alpheus (1905- , Tampa, FL) poet

  Make Way for Happiness. Boston: Christopher,
  1932.
  Sepia Vistas. New York: Exposition Press, 1941.

Attended Fisk University (M.A.). Authored *American
Negro Poetry, 1900-1918: A Critical Evaluation*.
Contributed to *Opportunity*.
[39]

Butler, Samuel S. (1835-1902, MS) poet

  Wit and Humor. Edward, MS: New Light Steam Press,
  1911.

Campbell, James Edwin (1867-1896, was born in
Pomeroy, Ohio, but worked in the South) editor,
educator, poet

  Driftings and Gleanings. Chicago: The Author,
  1888.
  Echoes from the Cabin and Elsewhere. Chicago: The
  Author, 1895.
  (Contributed poems to the *A.M.E. Church Review*,
  1889, and *Poets of America*, 1890)

Attended school in Pomeroy, Ohio. Worked as editor of
the *West Virginia Enterprise* in Kanawha County, West
Virginia (1887-1890); principal of a school in Point
Pleasant, West Virginia (1890-1891); president of
West Virginia Colored Institute--West Virginia State
College (1891-1893); staff member of the *Chicago
Times Herald*(1893-1896). Contributed to such

newspapers as the *Chronicle, Record, InterOcean, Tribune, Illustrated Push*--all Chicago area newspapers.
[36]

Cannon, David Wadsworth, Jr. (1910-1938, born in New Brunswick, New Jersey, but taught at Virginia State College) teacher, musician, poet

  Black Labor Chants and Other Poems. New York: The National Council on Religion in Higher Education, 1939.

Attended Cranford, New Jersey public school, Hillsdale College in Michigan (B.S., 1931), University of Michigan (M.A., 1932), Columbia University (died before completion of Ph.D.). Received the Julius Rosenwald Fellowship (1937) and the National Council on Religion in Higher Education Fellowship for doctoral study in educational psychology (1937). Taught at Virginia State College, Petersburg, Virginia--Assistant Professor of Psychology and Education (1932-1936).
[Foreword in *Black Labor Chants*]

Carmicheal, Waverly Turner (Snow Hill, AL) poet

  From the Heart of a Folk. A Book of Songs. Boston: Cornhill, 1918.

Carter, Herman J.D. (worked in Washington, D.C.) newspaper correspondent, writer

  The Scottsboro Blues. Nashville: The Mahlon Publishing Co., 1933.

Newspaper correspondent for the Associated Negro Press, the Scott Newspaper Syndicate, the *Pittsburgh Courier*, and the Afro-American newspapers. Federal Government employee; founded *The American Negro Mind Magazine* and "First Novel Syndicate," both of which were suspended when he entered WWII.
[38]

Cheriot, Henri (FL) novelist

  Black Ink. Orlando, FL: Henri CHeriot Publishing Co., 1917.

Chestnutt, Charles W. (1858-1932, Cleveland, OH, but

grew up in Fayetteville, North Carolina) lawyer,
stenographer, journalist, and fiction writer

  *The Wife of His Youth and Other Stories of the
  Color Line*. Boston: Houghton Mifflin, 1899.
  The Conjure Woman. New York: Houghton Mifflin,
  1899.
  The House Behind the Cedars. Boston: Houghton
  Mifflin, 1900.
  The Marrow of Tradition. Boston: Houghton
  Mifflin, 1901.
  The Colonel's Dream. New York: Doubleday, Page
  and Company, 1905.

Taught in the public schools of North Carolina at
sixteen; appointed principal of the State Normal
School in Fayetteville at age twenty-three. Worked as
newspaperman and court stenographer in Cleveland
until he passed the Ohio Bar in 1887. His first
short story "The Goophered Grapevine" appeared in the
Atlantic Monthly in August 1887. Awards included the
Spingarn Gold Medal for his "pioneer work as a
literary artist depicting the life and struggle of
Americans of Negro descent." His last work, an
article, was published in *Colophon*, in 1931.
[36, 42]

Christian, Ethel L. Perry (1886- , LaGrange, TN)
dramatist

  American Sunbursts.

Educated at Lemoyne Institute.
[57]

Christian, Marcus Bruce (1900- , worked in New
Orleans) library assistant and poet

  (Articles and poems in *Crisis, Opportunity, Phylon,
  The Louisiana Weekly, Negro Voices*)

Worked as supervisor of the Dillard University Negro
History Unit of the Federal Writers Project; Library
assistant at Dillard. Awarded a Rosenwald Fellowship
for further study of the history of the Negro in
Louisiana. Published *High Ground; a Collection of
Poems* in 1958.
[39]

Clarke, John Henrik (1915- , Union Springs, AL)
professor, editor, essayist, biographer, poet

Rebellion in Rhyme.   Prairie City, IL: Decker
Press, 1948.

Attended secondary school in New York City; studied
at New York University (1948-1952), New School of
Social Research (1956-1958), University of Ibadan-
Nigeria, University of Ghana-Accra.   Received the
honorary L.H.D. from the University of Denver (1970).
Helped to develop African Study Center, New School
for Social Research.   Edited *Freedomways* (associate
editor), *Harlem Quarterly* (co-founder and associate
editor), *Negro History Bulletin* (Book Reviews
editor); wrote features and/or reviews for *Pittsburgh
Courier*, *Ghana Evening News*, *Presence Africaine*.
Army Air Force (1941-1945); Professor (adjunct) at
Hunter College in New York City, and (visiting)
Cornell University; teacher, Malverne High School,
Long Island, New York; director of first U.S. African
Heritage Exposition (1959), director of Heritage
Teaching Program, HARYOU-ACT (1964-1969).   Awards
include Carter G. Woodson Award for Creative
Contribution in Editing (1968), Natra Citation for
Meritorious Achievement in Educational Television
(1969), Carter G. Woodson Award for Distinguished and
Outstanding Work in Teaching of History (1971).
Nonfiction works include *The Lives of Great African
Chiefs* (1958), *Harlem, A Community in Transition*
(1964, 1969), *William Styron's Nat Turner: Ten Black
Writers Respond* (1968--edited), *Malcolm X, the Man
and His Times* (1969), *Slave Trade and Slavery* (1970--
with Vincent Harding), *Black Titan; W.E. DuBois*
(1970), *Marcus Garvey and the Vision of Africa* (1974--
with Amy Jacques Garvey), *Black Families in the
American Economy* (1974--edited), *The Prescriber*
(1975).
[2, 42]

Clark, Peter Wellington (1914- , Alexandria, LA)
teacher, folklorist, poet

Educated at Blessed Sacrament School (1922-1927);
Xavier Preparatory School in New Orleans (1927-1931),
Valencia C. Jones Normal School (1931-1933), Xavier
University (B.A., 1938), University of Michigan
(Summer, 1939), Xavier University (M.A., 1942).
Founder and first editor of *Xavier Alumni Voice*, and
editor of three armed forces publications--*Vanguard*,
Retort, and *Attack*; foreman at Delta Shipyard;
salesman of stenographic supplies, army. Worked in
the school system of New Orleans. Authored *Delta*

Shadows, a pictorial study of New Orleans; edited *Arrows of Gold,* an anthology of Catholic verse. Awards include a gold medal award from the Catholic Press Association (1939).
[38, 42]

Clem, Charles Douglas (1876-1934, Johnson City, TN) mason, lecturer, article writer, poet

  Rhymes of a Rhymster. Edmond, OK: Author, 1901.
  A Little Souvenir. (No imprint, 1908).
  Booker T. Washington, A Poem. (n.d.)

Attended school in Tennessee, Oklahoma (about 1891, completed common school), Greeneville College in Tennessee (B.S.,1898--no record of attendance can be located). Taught school in Oklahoma; worked a short time with Santa Fe Railroad, head of linoleum and rug department of the Rosenthal Department of Chanute, Kansas (1909-1926). Books include *Oklahoma, Her People and Professions* (1892), *Fourteen Years in Metaphysics* (1913), and *The Upas Tree of Kansas,* (1917). Edited the *Western World in Oklahoma* (1901-1902) and *Coffeyville* (Kansas) *Vindicator.* He contributed articles to *The Kansas City Post* and the *African Times and Orient Review.*
[52]

Clifford, Carrie Williams (Washington, D.C.) educator, poet

  Race Rhymes. Washington, D.C.: Pendleton, 1911.
  The Widening Light. Boston: Walter Reid Co.,
     1922.
[19, 34]

Coffin, Frank Barbour (1871-1951, Holly Springs, MS) pharmacist, poet

  Coffin's Poems with Ajax's Ordeal. Little Rock,
     AS: Colored Advocate, 1897.
  Factum Factorum (poem). New York: New Haven
     Press, 1947.
[52]

Coleman, Jamye H., poet

  Songs of My Soul (poems)
  Cries from the Cross (Meditations)

Attended   Fisk   University--Community   School   of
Religion. Produced several plays.
[38]

Collins, Leslie Morgan (1914- , Alexandria, LA) poet

  Exile, a Book of Verse. Atlanta: The B.F. Logan
    Press, 1938.

Attended   Dillard   (M.A.,   1936),   Western   Reserve
University (Ph.D., 1945).   Professor of English at
Fisk   University   (Nashville,   Tennessee). Senior book
reviewer for the *Nashville Tennessean.*
[28, 44]

Cook,   Mercer   (1903-   , Washington, D.C.) music
composer, poet

  (Published numerous   articles and poems in journals
  and magazines)

Attended public   school in Washington, D.C. and New
York City, Amherst (B.A., 1925), University of Paris
(Diploma,   1926), Brown University (M.A., 1931; Ph.D.,
1936);   studied   in   Paris,   French West Indies,
University of Havana.   Received the John W. Simpson
Fellowship to the Sorbonne (1925-1926), a fellowship
from   the   General   Education Board to study in Paris
(1934),   the   Rosenwald Fellowship for study in Paris
and the French West Indies (1938), and a General
Education Board Fellowship to attend the University
of Havana (1942-1943). Taught at North Carolina A&T,
Howard   University, and Atlanta University (1936-
).   His   articles   and reviews have been published in
Vendredi, a Paris weekly newspaper (1938). Served on
the   editorial   boards   of *Phylon* and the *Journal of
Negro History*.   His   first   book, *Le Noir; Morceaux
Chosis de Vingt-neuf Francais Celebres* was published
in 1934.
[50]

Cooper, Anna Julia (1859-1964, GA) educator, author

  A Voice From the South. Xenia, Ohio: 1892.
  Christmas Plays. (no imprint.)

Received Ph.D. from the Sorbonne in Paris. Taught at
Dunbar High School in Washington, D.C.

Corbett, Maurice (1839-1920, Yanceyville, NC) poet

The Harp of Ethiopia. Nashville, TN: National
Baptist Publishing Board, 1914.

Attended   Shaw   University.   Served   in   the   North
Carolina   Legislature.   Clerk   in   Census   Bureau,
Washington, D.C. until stricken with paralysis in
1919.
[19, 30]

Cotter,   Joseph   S.,   Jr.   (1895-1919, Louisville, KY)
poet

  The Band of Gideon and Other Lyrics.   Boston:
  Cornhill, 1918.

Attended Louisville Central High (diploma, 1911),
Fisk (until TB treatment was needed). One book of
poems and one of one-act plays remained unpublished
at his death.
[56]

Cotter,   Joseph   Seamon,   Sr.   (1861-1949,   Nelson
County, Bardstown, KY) ragpicker, tobacco stemmer,
brickyard   hand,   whisky   distiller,   teamster,
prizefighter, teacher, poet, dramatist

  A Rhyming. Louisville, KY: New South Publishing,
  1895.
  Links of Friendship. Louisville, KY: The Bradley
  and Gilbert Co., 1898.
  A White Song and a Black One. Louisville, KY: The
  Bradley and Gilbert Co., 1909.
  Negro Tales. 1912. rpt. Miami: Mnemosyne
  Publishing Co., 1969.
  Collected Poems of Joseph S. Cotter. New York:
  Henry Harrison, 1938.
  *Sequel to the "Pied Pier of Hamelin" and Other
  Poems*. New York: Harrison, 1939.
  Caleb, the Degenerate. New York: Harrison, 1940.

Quit school at 8 (3rd Grade); attended school at
night and received his diploma at 23. Picked up rags
in the streets and worked in tobacco factories and
brickyards;   distiller;   teamster.   His   unpublished
works   include   "Life's   Dawn   and   Dusk,"   "Caesar
Driftwood and Other One Act Plays," and "My Mother
and Her Family."
[56]

Cuney, Waring (1906- , Washington, D.C.) teacher, poet

Attended public schools in Washington, D.C., Howard University, Lincoln University, and the New England Conservatory of Music. He has written two books of poetry, *Puzzles* (1960) and *Storefront Church* (1973). Co-edited the volume *Lincoln University Poets* (1954). Received one half of first and one half of second prizes in *Opportunity*'s 1926 literary contest for poem, "No Images." Contributed to *Opportunity* and other magazines and journals. Some poems set to music and recorded on album, "Southern Exposure."
[20]

Cuthbert, Marion V. (worked in AL) dean, poet

   Songs of Creation. New York: Women's Press, 1949.

Dean of Women at Talledega in the 1920s. Contributed to *Opportunity*. Published a biography, *Juliette Derricote* (1933).

Curtwright, Wesley (1910- , Brunswick, GA) poet

   (Contributed to *Opportunity* and the *Messenger*, and to anthologies including *Caroling Dusk*)

Attended Harlem Academy, among other schools--at intervals.
[39]

Danner, Margaret (1915- , Pryorsburg, KY) poet

   (Poems in *Poetry: Magazine of Verse*, 1952)

Received the John Hay Whitney Opportunity Award for a trip to Africa, and an award from Poets in Concert. Published a collection of verse, *Iron Lace*, in 1968. Poet-in-residence at Virginia Union University in Richmond (1970).
[7]

Davis, Daniel W. (1862-1913, NC) poet

   Idle Moments; Containing Emancipation and Other Poems. Baltimore, MD: The Educators of Morgan College, 1895.
   'Weh Down Souf, and Other Poems. Cleveland, OH: Helman-Taylor Co., 1897.

Attended public school in Richmond, Virginia. Taught
in the schools of Virginia for 33 years, conducting
summer normal schools throughout Virginia, West
Virginia and the Carolinas. Pastored at the Second
Baptist Church in Richmond from 1896 until his
death. Wrote the Exposition ode for the opening of
the Negro building at the Atlanta Exposition of 1895.
[10, 52]

Davis, Ossie (1922- , Cogsdell, GA) actor, director,
playwright

   Goldbrickers of 1944, play
   Alice in Wonder, one-act play, 1953

Attended Central High School in Waycross, Georgia,
Howard University (1938-1941), and Columbia
University. Awarded the Frederick Douglass Award
(1970), entry into the Black Filmmakers Hall of Fame
(1974), Actors Equity Paul Robeson Citation (1975).
Has written a number of plays and scripts, and has
performed on television and in theatrical
productions.
[37, 42]

Delaney, Clarissa M. Scott (1901-1927, Tuskegee
Institute, AL) teacher, poet

   (In *The Poetry of the Negro* and *Opportunity*)

Graduated from Wellesley College. Teacher in
Washington, D.C. Appointed director of the Joint
Committee on Negro Child Study in New York City
(1926). Daughter of Emmett J. Scott, secretary to
Booker T. Washington.
[1, 7]

Delaney, Martin Robinson (1812-1885, Charleston, W
VA) author, publisher, soldier, physician, novelist

   Blake, or the Huts of America. 1859. rpt. New York:
   Arno Press of the New York Times, 1969.

Attended elementary school in Chamberburg, VA;
studied in AME Church high school, beginning at 19;
studied medicine with doctor, becoming qualified to
practice as cupper, leecher, bleeder--began his study
of medicine at Harvard University Medical School in
1850. Published *The Mystery in Pittsburgh*--the first
Negro newspaper west of the Allegheny Mountains,

served as co-editor with Frederick Douglass of the *North Star* in Rochester, New York. Nonfiction includes *The Condition, Elevation, Emigration and Destiny of the Colored People of the United States, Politically Considered* (1852), *Official Report of the Niger Valley Exploring Party* (1861), *Principia of Ethnology: The Orgin of Race and Color* (1879).
[36]

Demby, William (1922- , born in Pittsburgh, PA, but spent youth and attended college in W VA) novelist

   Beetlecreek. New York: Rhinehart, 1950.

Attended West Virginia State College before being drafted into the Army, then Fisk University (B.A., 1947), and later the University of Rome. Contributed to the Army's *Stars and Stripes*, and wrote for student publications while at Fisk. Contributed to *Harper's, Reporter*, and *Holiday*. Published novels, *The Catacombs* (1965) and *Love Story Black* (1978).
[33]

Dett, Robert Nathaniel (1882-1943, born in Canada, but worked at Hampton Institute, VA) pianist, composer, poet

   Album of the Heart, 1911.

Educated at Oliver Willis Halstead Conservatory of Music (Locksport, New York), and Oberlin Conservatory of Music; took courses at Columbia University, the University of Pennsylvania, Harvard University, the American Conservatory of Music of Chicago; the Eastman School of Music of the University of Rochester; and other schools in Europe. Worked at Lane College in Tennessee (1908-1911), Lincoln Institute in Missouri (1913-?), and Hampton Institute in Virginia, becoming chairman of the music department in 1926, director of music at Bennett College (Greensboro, North Carolina), did chorus work with the USO shortly before his death. Composed a number of musical works, including "The Magnolia Suite," "In the Bottoms," "The Chariot Jubilee," "The Ordering of Moses," and "America the Beautiful." Published two books of music: *Religious Folk Songs of the Negro* and the *Dett Collection of Spirituals*. Honors include the Bowdoin Prize at Harvard for his essay "The Emancipation of Negro Music" (1920), the Francis Boot Prize for a motet, "Don't Be a Weary

Traveller," and the Harmon award for achievement in music (1927).
[37]

Dickerson, Noy Jasper (1892- , Elkhorn, W VA) educator, poet

  Original Poetry. Bluefield, W VA: Author, 1927.
  A Scrapbook. Boston: The Christopher Publishing
    House, 1931.

Attended school in Bluefield, West Virginia, Bluefield State Teachers College, and North Carolina A&T. Worked at a number of schools in West Virginia.
[57]

Dinkins, Charles R. (SC) minister of the AME Zion Church, poet

  Lyrics of Love. Columbia, SC: The State Co.,
    1904.
[56]

Dismond, H. Binga (1891- , Richmond, VA) therapist, celebrated track star, poet

  We Who Would Die and Other Poems. New York:
    Malliett and Co., 1943.

Director of the Department Physical Therapy at Harlem Hospital in New York. Cited by President Stenio Vincent of Haiti for his work following the Dominican Massacre of 1937--Chevalier of the National Order of Honor and Merit of Haiti.
[Foreword, 38]

Dodson, Owen (1914- , born in Brooklyn but worked in Atlanta, GA and Washington, D.C.) professor, novelist, dramatist, poet

  Including Laughter, 1936
  Gargoyles in Florida, 1936
  Divine Comedy, 1938
  The Garden of Time, 1939
  Amistad, 1939
  The Southern Star, 1940
  Doomsday Tale, 1941
  Everybody Join Hands, 1942
  Someday We're Gonna Tear the Pillars Down, 1942
  Freedom the Banner, 1942

The Ballad of Dorie Miller, 1942
New World A-Coming, 1944
Bayou Legend, 1946
The Third Fourth of July (with Countee Cullen),
1946
Powerful Long Ladder. New York: Farrar, Straus,
1946.

Educated at Bates College (B.A., 1936) and Yale
University (M.F.A., 1939). Directed drama at Atlanta
University (1938-1942), and at Spellman College (1938-
1942). Began work as director of Howard Players in
1947, and became chairman of the drama department at
Howard University in 1960. Awarded a General
Education Board Fellowship (1938, 1939), a Rosenwald
Fellowship (1944), a Guggenheim grant (1953) for a
year of writing in Italy, a Paris Review short story
contest prize (1955), and the Maxwell Anderson Verse
Play Award (1940). In 1949, he took the Howard
University Players, sponsored by the State
Department, on tour to Scandinavia and Germany. Co-
founded the Negro Ensemble Company. Has written a
number of plays since 1953.
[11, 37, 42]

Dreer, Herman (1889-   , Washington, D.C.) educator,
editor, novelist

   The Immediate Jewel of His Soul. St. Louis: The
   St. Louis Argus Publishing Co., 1919.

Attended Washington D.C. public schools, Bowdoin
College (A.B.), Virginia Theological Seminary (A.M.),
University of Illinois, and Columbia University.
Published *The Tie That Binds* in 1958.
[57]

DuBois, William Edward Burghardt (1868-1963, born in
Great Barrington, Massachusetts but worked in the
South) professor, editor, novelist

   The Quest of the Silver Fleece. 1911. rpt. College
   Park, MD: McGrath Publishing Co., 1969.
   Dark Princess. 1928. rpt. New York: Harcourt,
   Brace, and Co., 1970.

Attended public school in Massachusetts, Fisk
University, Harvard (B.A., 1890; M.A., 1891; Ph.D.,
1895), and the University of Berlin. Professor of
Latin and Greek at Wilberforce and of Economics,

head of the department of sociology at Atlanta
University (1933-), and professor at the University
of Pennsylvania. Organized the Niagara Conference
(1905), co-founded the NAACP (1909-1910). Edited the
Crisis (1910-1934) and *Phylon* (1940-1944). Headed
the NAACP's Special Research Department and Publicity
(1944-1948). Nonfiction works include *Suppression of
African Slave Trade* (1896), *The Philadelphia Negro*
(1899), *The Souls of Black Folk* (1903), *John Brown*
(1909), *The Negro* (1915), *Darkwater* (1920), *The Gift
of Black Folk* (1924), *Black Reconstruction* (1935),
Black Folk, Then and Now (1939), *Dusk of Dawn* (1940).
Also, published *The Ordeal of Mansart* (1957),
Mansart Builds a School (1959), and *Worlds of Color*
(1961).
[36, 42, 45]

Dunbar, Alice Ruth Moore (See Nelson, Alice Ruth
Moore Dunbar.)

Echols, Carl (Atlanta, GA) violinist, poet, writer

Taught school, did manual labor, was a violinist, and
a political asperant. Co-founded and co-authored the
first Negro newspaper in Pasadena, California.
Published a volume of verse.
[57]

Edmonds, Randolph (1900- , Lawrenceville, VA)
professor, dramatist

   Shades and Shadows. Boston: Meador Publishing Co.,
   1930.
   Six Plays for the Negro Theatre. Boston: Walter
   Baker Co., 1934.
   The Land of Cotton and Other Plays. Washington,
   D.C.: Associated Publishers, 1952.
   *Earth and Stars: A Problem Play Concerning Negro
   and White Leadership in the South.* Tallahassee:
   n.p.,1961.

Attended St. Paul Normal and Industrial School of
Lawrenceville, Virginia, Oberlin College (B.A.,
1926), Columbia University (M.A., 1932), Yale
University (one year of further study), Dublin
University, and London School of Speech Training and
Dramatic Arts. Instructor of English and drama at
Morgan College, professor of drama at Dillard
University in New Orleans and Florida A&M University
in Tallahassee. Founded the Negro Intercollegiate

Drama   Association   (1930),   and   the   Southern
Association   of   Drama and Speech Arts (1935). Awarded
honorary   Litt.D.   from   Bethune-Cookman   College,
selected,   in   1958, to take his FAMU Playmakers Guild
to   tour   Africa   under   the   President   of the United
States'   Special   International   Program   for Cultural
Presentations--nomination   was   made   by   the American
National   Theatre Academy; selected again, in 1963, to
tour   Western   European countries.   Referred to as the
"Dean   of   the   Black   Academic   Theatre."   Wrote more
than 40 plays.
[40, 37]

Fabio,   Sarah   Webster (1928- , Nashville, TN) critic,
educator, poet

Taught   at   Meritt College in California.   Published *A
Mirror: A   Soul*(1969),   *Black   Is   a   Panther   Caged*
(1972),   and   *Rainbow   Signs*   (1974).   Poems   in
anthologies and magazines.
[1]

Felton,   Haleemon   Shaik   (1913-   ,   LA)   educator,
dramatist

   (In Peter Wellington Clark's *Arrows of Gold*)

Attended   secondary   school   in New Orleans, Valena C.
Jones   Normal   School   (teacher's   certificate,   1932),
and   college, Xavier (B.A., 1940).   Unpublished dramas
include: *House   of   Eternal   Darkness* (New Orleans,
Dillard,   1941),   *Backstage* (New Orleans, Xavier, 1933,
1937),   and   *Drifting   Souls*   (New   Orleans, St. Peter
Claver Auditorium, 1933).
[50]

Fernandis,   Sarah   Collins   (1863-   ,   Baltimore, MD)
social worker, poet

   (Poems in *The Southern Workman*)

Graduated   from   Hampton University (1882).   Served as
a   social   worker   under   the   Woman's Home Missionary
Society   of   Boston,   teaching   in   Tennessee   and
Florida.   Taught   in the public schools of Baltimore.
While   a   social   worker,   established   model homes in
Washington's Bloodfield   and   East   Greenwich,   Rhode
Island.   Also worked as a social investigator.
[56]

Fields, Maurice (1915-1938, Jacksonville, FL) poet

  The Collected Poems of Maurice C. Fields. New
    York: The Exposition Press, 1940.
  Testament of Youth. New York: Pegasus Publishing
    Co., 1941.

Attended Manual Training High School in Brooklyn, New
York, Brooklyn College (B.S., 1937). Drowned just
before he was to enter Columbia University.
[50]

Finch, Amanda (AL) novelist

  Black Trail: A Novella of Love in the South. New
  York: William-Frederick Press, 1951.

Finch, Giles (Birmingham, AL) miner, poet

  A Collection of 75 Original Poems. Author:
  Birmingham, 1955.
    (All were written before 1955.)
[9]

Fisher, Leland Milton (1875-1905, Humboldt, TN) poet

  (In Kerlin's *Negro Poets*)

Died of TB at 35. Credited with an unpublished
volume of poems.
[34]

Fisher, Rudolph (1897-1934, Washington, D.C.)
teacher, physician, novelist

  The Walls of Jericho. New York: Knopf, 1928.
  *The Conjure Man Dies, A Mystery Tale of Dark
    Harlem.* Covice-Friede, 1932.

Attended Brown University (A.B., and A.M., 1920),
Howard University Medical School (M.D., 1924).
Worked as a biology teacher before practicing
medicine in New York City. Contributed to *Crisis,
Atlantic Monthly, Story Magazine, and Survey Graphic.*
[57]

Flanagan, Thomas Jefferson (1890-1965, Stewart
County, GA) minister, poet

  By the Pine Knot Torches. Atlanta: The Dickcut
    Co., 1921.

The Harvest Hymn. Atlanta: Privately Printed,
  n.d.
The Road to Mount McKeithan. Atlanta: Independent
  Publishers Corporation, 1927.
Smilin' Thru the Corn, and Other Verse. Atlanta:
  Independent Publishers Corporation, 1927.
The Canyons of Providence. Atlanta: The
  Author, 1941.

Educated in the public schools of Bluff Springs,
Georgia, Payne High School, Cuthbert, Georgia, Morris
Brown College, and Atlanta University (A.B.).
Received honorary D. Ph. from Paul Quinn College in
Waco, Texas. Contributed to *Atlanta World, Macon
Daily Telegraph*, *Negro World* and the *Atlanta
Constitution*, and edited the *Georgia African
Methodist* (Morris Brown) and *Scroll* (Atlanta
University). Worked as principal at Lumpkin High
School in Georgia and also as a railway mail clerk.
Published a book of hymns, *The Blood of Jesus* (1964).
[57]

Fleming, Sarah Lee Brown (GA) poet, novelist

  Clouds of Sunshine. Boston: Cornhill, 1920.
  Hope's Highway. New York: The Neale Publishing
  Co., 1918.

Floyd, Silas X (1869- , GA) fiction writer

  Floyd's Flowers. 1905. rpt. New York: AMS Press,
  1970.
  *Short Stories for Colored People, Both Old and
  Young*. 1920.

Graduated from Atlanta University in 1891 (M.S.), and
Morris Brown College (D.D.). Served as principal of
public school in Augusta, Georgia; pastor of
Tabernacle Baptist Church in Augusta. Contributed
articles to a number of magazines. Authored other
books--nonfiction: *Life of Charles T. Walker, D.D.*
(1902), and *A Sketch of Rev. C.T. Walker* (1892).
[Introduction to Floyd's Flowers]

Ford, Nick Aaron (1904-1982, Ridgeway, SC)
professor, literary critic, consultant, poet

  Songs from the Dark: Original Poems. Boston:
  Meador, 1940.

Attended Benedict College in Columbia, South Carolina
(B.A.; M.A., 1934) and the University of Iowa (Ph.D.,
1945). Taught in Florida, Texas, Oklahoma,
Massachusetts, and Maryland (Department chairperson,
Morgan State College (1947-1970); Alain Locke
Professor of Black Studies, Morgan State (1970-1973).
Black Studies consultant, U.S. Office of Education,
Ford Foundation and National Endowment for the
Humanities. Director and professor at Union
Graduate School, Center for Minority Studies,
Brookings Institution, Washington, D.C. (1976-1979).
Nonfiction works include *The Contemporary Negro Novel*
(1936), *Basic Skills for Better Writing* (co-edited
with Waters Turpin, 1959), and *American Culture in
Literature* (1967). Edited *Baltimore Afro-American:
Best Short Stories by Afro-American Writers, 1925-
1950; A Study in Race Relations* (1950). Published
Seeking a Newer World in 1983.
[42]

Fordham, Mary Weston (SC) poet

   Magnolia Leaves. Charleston, S.C.: Walker, Evans
   and Cogswell Co., 1897.

Forster, Estelle Ancrum (1887- , Wilmington, NC)
musician-director, playwright

   *A Dream of Enchantment (a musical play in three
   acts).* Boston: Theo. Presser, 1926.

Attended Benedict College and the New England
Conservatory of Music, Boston. Founder-director of
Ancrum School of Music, Boston. Authored *Piano
Composition* (1926), and *Ancrum School Course in Sight
Singing* (1926).
[57]

Fortune, Timothy Thomas (1856-1928, Marianna, FL)
journalist, teacher, poet

   Dreams of Life: Miscellaneous Poems. New York:
   Fortune and Peterson, 1905.

Attended Howard University. Worked as a page in the
Florida Senate and as a printer's devil for four
newspapers in Florida during his teen years, as a
clerk in the Jacksonville post office, as private
secretary to a Florida congressman, as a mail route
agent of the Railway mail service in Florida, as an

inspector of customs in Delaware, as a teacher in Florida before getting into the newspaper business. Founder of the *New York Age* and the *New York Globe* and the *New York Freeman*; wrote for the *People's Advocate*, *New York Sun*, *Boston Transcript*, *Norfolk Journal and Guide*; edited *Negro World*. Nonfiction works include *Black and White: Land, Labor and Politics in the South* (1884) and *The Negro in Politics* (1885).
[36, 42, 53]

Fowler, Charles Henry (1837-1908) novelist

   Historical Romance of the American Negro.
   Baltimore, MD: Press of Thomas and Evans, 1902.

Franklin, James Thomas (TN) poet

   Jessamine Poems. Memphis, TN: Tracy Printing, 1900.
   Mid-Day Gleanings, a Book for Home and Holiday Reading. Memphis, TN: Tracy Printing and Stationery, 1893.

Gholson, E., minister, author, poet

   Musings of a Minister. Boston: Christopher, 1943.
   From Jerusalem to Jericho. Boston: Chapman and Grimes, 1943.

Gilbert, Mercedes (FL) actor, novelist, poet

   Aunt Sara's Wooden God. Boston: Christopher, 1938.
   Selected Gems of Poetry, Comedy and Drama. Boston: Christopher, 1931.

Performed on Broadway in such plays as *Mulatto*, *Green Pastures*, *The Little Foxes*, *The Male Animal*, and *The Searching Wind*. Career ranged from vaudeville to conducting her own one-woman theatre. Songwriter-- "The Decatur Street Blues" and "The Also Ran Blues." Radio performances including her own program. Authored several books.

Gilmore, F. Grant, novelist, poet

   Masonic and Other Poems. The Author, n.p., 1908.
   The Problem; a Military Novel. 1915. rpt. College Park, MD.: McGrath Publishing Co., 1969.

Gloster, Hugh (1911- , Brownville, TN) professor, editor

Educated at Howe Institute, Manassas High School, Lemoyne College (completed high school and junior college, 1929), Morehouse (B.A., 1931), Atlanta University (M.A., 1933), and New York University (Ph.D., 1943). Taught at Lemoyne College (1933-1941) and Hampton Institute (professor/department chairperson (1946-1947). President of Morehouse College (1967-). Founder of College Language Association. Co-editor of *The Brown Thrush: Anthology of Verse by Negro Students* (1932, 1935). Contributing editor of *Phylon* (1948-1953). Nonfiction works include *Negro Voices in American Fiction* (1948, 1965), *My Life, My Country, My World: College Readings for Modern Living* (1952), *The Negro Novel in America* (1948). Awarded the General Education Board Fellowship (1938-1939) and an Alpha Phi Alpha Fraternity fellowship for dissertation research in 1940. Contributed articles to *Opportunity* and *Phylon*.
[42]

Gordon, Charles Benjamin William (1861- , Colerain, NC) minister, orator, journalist, poet

Attended Thomas Nixon School in Roanoke Island, Virginia. Pastored in Florida, Alabama, and Texas. Served as president of the Florida Baptist Academy (1892).
[12]

Graham, Lorenz Bell (1902- , New Orleans, LA) lecturer, teacher, probation officer, juvenile writer

  How God Fix Jonah. New York: Reynal, 1946.
  Every Man Heart Lay Down. New York: Crowell, 1946.
  God Wash the World and Start Again. New York: Crowell, 1946.
  Tales of Momolu. NY: Reynal, 1946.

Attended UCLA, Columbia University, University of Paris, Virginia Union University (B.A., 1936), and New York University. Worked as a teacher and missionary in Liberia (1924-1928), lecturer and fundraiser for the Foreign Mission Board of the National Baptist Convention (1929-1932), teacher in Richmond, Virginia (1933-1935), camp education

advisor for Civilian Conservation Corps in Virginia
and Pennsylvania (1936-1942), manager of public
housing in Newport News, Virginia (1943-1945), free
lance writer, and building contractor in Long Island,
New York (1946-1949), social worker teacher with
Queens Federation of Churches in New York (1950-
1957), probation officer in Los Angeles California
(1958-1966, teacher at California State University
(1970-   ). Honors include the Thomas A. Edison
Citation (1956), Charles W. Follett Award (1958),
L.H.D. from Virginia Union University (1983).
Published *Southtown* (1958) and *The Story of Jesus*
(1955).
[42]

Griggs, Sutton (1872-1933, Chatfield, TX--worked in
the South) Baptist clergyman, novelist

   Imperium in Imperio. 1899. rpt. Miami: Mnemosyne,
   1969.
   Overshadowed. 1901. rpt. New York: AMS Press,
   1970.
   Unfettered. 1902. rpt. New York: AMS Press, 1970.
   The Hindered Hand; or the Reign of the
   Repressionist. 1905. rpt. Miami: Mnemosyne,
   1969.
   Pointing the Way. 1908. rpt. New York: AMS Press,
   1970.
   Wisdom's Call. 1911. Miami: Mnemosyne, 1969.

Attended Dallas Public schools, Bishop College (B.A.,
1890) and Richmond Theological Seminary--Virginia
Union University (between 1890 and 1893). Pastored
in Virginia and Tennessee. Authored many pamphlets.
Nonfiction works include *Life's Demands, or According
to Law* (1916), *Guide to Racial Greatness* (1923),
Kingdom Builders' Manual (1924), and *Triumph of the
Simple Virtues, or the Life Story of John L. Webb*
(1926).
[36]

Grimke, Angelina Weld (1880-1958, worked in
Washington, D.C.) teacher, playwright, poet

   Rachel; A Play in Three Acts. 1920. rpt. College
   Park, MD: McGrath Publishing Co., 1969.
   (Poetry in Arna Bontemps' *Caroling Dusk, Black and
   White, The Crisis, Opportunity*, and other books and
   magazines)

Educated at Carleton Academy in Northfield, Minnesota, Cushing Academy in Asburnham, Massachusetts, Girls' Latin School in Boston, and Boston Normal School of Gymnastics. Taught in Washington D.C. at Armstrong Manual Training School and at Dunbar High School.
[38]

Gunner, Mary Frances (1894- , Lexington, KY) teacher, YWCA secretary, dramatist

The Light of a Woman, a pageant. (n.d.)

Attended Middlebury College (1911-1912), Howard University (A.B., 1915), and Columbia University (A.M., 1930). Teacher (1915-1918); General Secretary of Montclair YWCA (1918-1921); general secretary of Ashland Place YWCA (1921-).
[57]

Hall, Josie B. (1867- , Waxahachie, TX, but lived in MS) teacher, writer

Attended Bishop College in Marshall, Texas. Taught in public schools of Canaan, Texas. Nonfiction includes *Moral and Mental Capsule for the Economic and Domestic Life of the Negro as a Solution of the Race Problem*, which contains some poetry.
[12]

Handy, William Christopher (1873-1958, Florence, AL)

Truth in Rhyme, and Miscellaneous Prose Compositions. U.S.: Caxton Press, 1928.

Attended Alabama A&M College and Fisk University. Worked as bandmaster for Mahara's Minstrels (1896- 1900), and music instructor at A&M College in Normal, Alabama (1900-1902). Formed Pace and Handy Music Company (publisher, 1913-1921). Published *Blues: An Anthology* (1926), *Father of the Blues* (autobiography, 1941) and *Unsung Americans Sung; A Treasury of the Blues* (1949).
[6, 37, 47]

Harper, Frances E. Watkins (1825-1911, Baltimore, MD) lecturer, abolitionist, novelist, poet

Poems on Miscellaneous Subjects. Boston: J.B. Yerrington and Sons, Printers, 1854.

> *Moses: A Story of the Nile*. Philadelphia:
>   Merrihew and Sons, Printers, 1869.
> *Poems*. Philadelphia: Merrihew and Sons, Printers,
>   1871.
> *Sketches of Southern Life*. Philadelphia: Merrihew,
>   1872.
> *The Martyr of Alabama and Other Poems*. 1872.
> *Iola Le Roy* or Shadows Uplifted. 1892. College
>   Park, MD: McGrath, 1969.
> *The Sparrow's Fall and Other Poems*. (n.d.)
> *Atlanta Offering Poems*. Philadelphia: The Author,
>   1895.
> *Poems*. 1898.
> *Light Beyond the Darkness*. (n.d.)
> *Idylls of the Bible*. Philadelphia: the Author,
>   1901.

Educated in the North in Pennsylvania and Ohio. Worked as an anti-slavery activist/lecturer (1867-1871) in every southern state except Texas and Arkansas.   Served as superintendent of Colored Work for the Women's Christian Temperance Union.
[36,45, 55,]

Harris, Leon R. (1866- , born in OH, but worked in the South) journalist, lecturer, poet, short story writer

> *The Steelmakers and Other War Poems*.   Portsmouth,
>   OH: T.C. Mcconnell Printery, 1918.
> *Locomotive Puffs from the Back Shop*.   Boston: B.
>   Humphries, 1946.
> *I Am a Railroad Man*. Los Angeles, CA: 1948.

Attended Berea College and Tuskegee Institute. Editor of the Richmond Indiana Blade, principal of Jamestown Colored School, and State Lecturer for the North Carolina Farmers' Cooperative Union. Published *Run, Zebra, Run!* in 1959.
[13]

Hawkins, Walter Everette (1886- , Warrenton, NC) postal worker, poet

> *Song of the Night Child*. Wilmington, NC: 1916.
> *Chords and Discords*. Boston: R.G. Badger, 1920.
> *The Child of the Night*. (n.d.)
> *The Black Soldiers*.(n.d.)
> *Where the Air of Freedom Is*. (n.d.)
> *Guardian*. (n.d.)

Love's Unchangeableness. (n.d.)
Too Much Religion. (n.d.)

Attended public school in Warrenton, North Carolina, and graduated from Kittrell College. Worked in the railway mail service.
[1, 34, 57]

Hayden, Robert (1913- , born in Detroit, Michigan, but worked in the South) professor, poet

   Heart-Shape in the Dust. Detroit: The Falcon
     Press, 1940.
   The Lion and the Archer. Nashville: Hemphill
     Press, 1948.

Attended Wayne State University and the University of Michigan (M.A.). Taught at the University of Michigan, Fisk University (1946-), University of Michigan (visiting professor, 1968), and the University of Louisville (visiting professor, 1969). Honors include the Hopwood Award from the University of Michigan (1938, 1942), a Rosenwald Fellowship (1947), and a Ford Foundation grant (1954), the Grand Prize for Poetry at the First World Festival of Negro Arts in Dakar, Senegal (1965). Editor and publisher of the Counterpoise Series, and editor of the Baha'i magazine *World Order*. Published *A Ballad of Remembrance* (1962), *Selected Poems* (1966), *Kaleidoscope* (1967), and *Words in the Mourning Time* (1970).
[7, 41, 45]

Hayes, Donald Jeffrey (1904- , Raleigh, NC) actor poet

   (In *Poetry of the Negro*, 1949)

Attended public school in Atlantic City and Pleasantville, New Jersey, and Chicago. Appeared in several Broadway productions in the 20s and 30s. Worked as a counselor for the New Jersey State Employment Service in Atlantic City. Contributed poetry to *Harper's Bazaar*, *Good Housekeeping*, and *This Week*.
[7, 17]

Heard, Josie Delphine Henderson (1861-1919, Salisbury, NC) teacher, poet

Morning Glories. Lancaster, PA: Speaker Printer,
  1890.

Educated in the public schools of Charlotte, North
Carolina, Scotia Seminary in Concord, North Carolina
and Bethany Institute in New York.. Taught in North
Carolina, South Carolina at Maysville, and Tennessee
at Covington.
[57]

Heard, William (1850-1937, Elbert County, GA) bishop,
poet

  From Slavery to Bishophric in the AME Church. 1924.
  rpt. New York: Arno Press, 1969.

Educated at Atlanta University, Columbia University,
R.E. Divinity School in West Philadephia, Allen
University in Columbia, South Carolina (D.D.). Was
AME minister/bishop, railway clerk, member of the
South Carolina House of Representatives, minister--
resident and Consul-General to Liberia.

Henderson, George Wylie (1904-1965, Warrior Stand,
AL) printer, novelist

  Ollie Miss. New York: Frederick A. Stokes Co.,
  1935.
  Jule. New York: Creative Age Press, Inc., 1946.

Learned printing at Tuskegee Institute. Worked as a
printer and short story writer for the New York *Daily
News.* Was working on his third novel at the time of
his death.
[3, 11]

Hill, Abram (1911- , Atlanta, GA) playwright

  Liberty Deferred (with John Silvera)
  Stealing Lightning, 1937
  Hell's Half Acre, 1938
  So Shall You Reap, 1938
  *Striver's Row: A Comedy About Sophisticated
  Harlem,* 1940
  Walk Hard, 1944
  Miss Mabel, 1951

Attended City College of New York (1930-1932),
Columbia University, Lincoln University (B.A., 1937),
and New School for Social Research, Atlanta

University.   Worked as Assistant New York State
Supervisor C.C.C. dramatic activities, drama critic
for *Amsterdam News* in New York, faculty member and
director of dramatics at Lincoln University,
researcher and consultant to Federal Writers Project
and Federal Theatre.   Co-founded the American Negro
Theatre.
[37]

Hill, John H. (-1936, Harewood, VA) novelist

  Princess Malah. Washington: Associated
  Publishers, 1933.
[*Introduction to Princess Malah].*

Hill, Julious (large sawmill town of the northeast
section of MS) singer, actor, poet, playwright

  The Up Reach. Meridian, MS: Tell Farmer, Printer
  and Binder, 1923.
  A Sooner Song. New York: Empire Publishing Co.,
  1935.
  A Song of Magnolia. Boston: Meador Publishing
  Co., 1937.

Attended Tuskegee, Alcorn, Morehouse, U.S. Naval
training, Langston University (A.B.). Conductor of
literary bureau in Tulsa, Oklahoma. Other works
include *Modern American Poetry* (co-author, 1934),
American Voices (co-author, 1935), *Who's Who in
American Poetry* (co-author), *Modern Troubadours* (co-
author, 1936), *Arkansas and Oklahoma Poets* (co-
author), *The Paehar Anthology of Verse* (co-
author).   Some verse printed in magazines,
newspapers and student periodicals.
[Introduction to Song of Magnolia]

Hill, Leslie Pinckney (1880-1960, Lynchburg, VA)
teacher, college president, poet

  The Wings of Oppression. Boston: Stratford, 1921.
  Toussaint L'Ouverture--A Dramatic History. Boston:
  Christopher, 1928.

Graduated from Harvard University (B.A., 1903; M.A.,
1904).   Honorary degrees: Lincoln University, Morgan
State College, Haverford College and Rhode Island
College of Education. Professor of English Education
at Tuskegee Institute (1904-1907), principal of
Manassas (VA) Industrial School (1907-1913), hospital

administrator in Philadephia, principal of the the
Insitute for Colored Youth--Cheyney Training School
for Teachers--(president) Cheyney State College in
Pennsylvania (1913-1951). Named president emeritus in
1951. Founded Camp Hope for underprivileged children
in Delaware County, Pennsylvania in 1944.
Contributed to *Crisis*.
[36, 42]

Hill, William Allyn (1908- , Baltimore, MD) educator,
poet

  (In *Lincoln Poets*)

Graduated from Lincoln (B.A., 1929) and then attended
the New England Conservatory of Music, Howard
University and the University of Berlin. Taught
vocal music at Howard University. Served in Signal
Corps during WWI. Served as Executive Secretary of
Washington D.C. branch oof the NAACP.
[20]

Holloway, Lucy Ariel Williams (1905- , Mobile AL)
director of music, poet

  Shape Them Into Dreams: Poems. New York:
   Exposition Press, 1955.

Attended Talladega and Fisk University. Director of
Music at North Carolina College for Negroes. Shared
one-half or first and one-half of second prize in
1926 *Opportunity* contest with poem, "Northboun."
[6]

Holloway, John Wesley (1865-1935, Flat Shoals,
Merriweather County, GA) clergyman, poet

  From the Desert. New York: Neal Co., 1919.
  Bandanas. Barber College, 1928.

Educated at Clark University, Atlanta; Fisk
University (A.B., 1894; B.D., 1904. A former Fisk
Jubilee Singer. Worked as assistant principal of a
Guthrie, Oklahoma High School and pastor of
congregational churches (1900-1904); clergyman in
Newark, New Jersey (1906-1910), Thebes, Georgia (1910-
1920), Anniston, Alabama (1920-1924); taught in
Anniston, Alabama (1927-1928). Served as associate
editor of *The Georgia Congregationalist*.
[6, 29, 57]

Holman, M.Carl (1919-   , Minter City, MS) writer, poet

Attended Lincoln University, the University of Chicago, and Yale University. Taught at Clark College. Worked as an information officer with the U.S. Commission on Civil Rights. Honors include The University of Chicago's John Billings Fiske Poetry Prize, and the Rosenwald Fellowship. Edited *The Atlanta Inquirer*.
[35]

Horton, George Moses (1797-1883, Northhampton County, NC) slave, poet

> *Hope of Liberty*. Raleigh, NC: Joseph Gales and Son, 1829.
> *Naked Genius*. Raleigh, NC: Wm. B. Smith and Co., Southern Field and Fireside Book Publishing House, 1865.
> *Poems by a Slave*. Philadephia. 1837.

Self-taught. Slave until his freedom was purchased by an abolitionist group. Literary career began around 1817 when he peddled fruit and vegetables at the University of Carolina--Chapel Hill: he sold his poetry to the students. In 1828, a benefactor had his poems "On Poetry and Musick," "Liberty and Slavery" and "Slavery" published in the *Lancaster Gazette*. Other poems published in Freedom's *Journal* (New York) the same year.
[2, 42, 45, 46, 55, 56]

Huff, William H. (Point Peter, Oglethorpe County, GA) pharmacist, lawyer, real estate and general insurance broker, poet, novelist

> *Sowing and Reaping*.(n.d.)
> *From Deep Within*. (n.d.)
> *I'm Glad I'm Who I Am*. (n.d.)
> *Low Ground of Sorrow*. (n.d.)

Schooled at Georgia Normal and Industrial Institute and Knox Institute in Athens, Georgia, National Medical University in Chicago, Chicago Law School (LL.B.), and John Marshall Law School (J.D.) . Practiced law: admitted to Indiana (1936) and Illinois (1946) Bars. Practiced before the United Circuit Court of Appeals and the U.S. Supreme Court. Practiced pharmacy.
[54]

Huntley,   Elizabeth   Maddox (Eatonville, GA) musician,
educator, dramatist
  (In anthologies)

Educated in Eatonville, Georgia, and at Morris Brown
College and Atlanta University.
[24]

Hurston,   Zora   Neale (1903-1960, Eatonville, FL)
anthropologist, folklorist, novelist

  Jonah's Gourd Vine. Philadephia: J.P. Lippincott,
    1934.
  Their Eyes Were Watching God. 1937. rpt. New York:
    Negro Universities Press, 1969.
  Moses, Man of the Mountain. Philadephia: J.B.
    Lippincott, 1939.
  Seraph on the Suwanee. New York: Charles
    Scribner's Sons, 1948.

Educated   at   Morgan   Academy of Morgan College,
Baltimore   Maryland   (high school); Howard University,
and   Barnard   College   (B.A., 1928), where she studied
under   Franz   Boas.   Honors include a Guggenheim
Fellowship for study of folklore in the Caribbean and
to   study   voodoo   in Haiti and Louisiana (1936, 1938)
and   a   Rosenwald   Foundation   Fellowship (1935).
Nonfiction   works   include *Mules and Men* (1935), *Tell
My   Horse* (1938), *Moses Man of the Mountain* (1939),
and *Dust Tracks on the Road* (autobiography, 1942).
Articles   appeared   in *Forum, Saturday Review of
Literature, American Mercury,* and *Saturday Evening
Post.*   Wrote   plays--*Color Struck, The First One*
(1927),   *Great   Day* (1927), *Mule Bone: A Comedy of
Negro Life in Three Acts* (written with Langston
Hughes,   1931),   *Polk County* (1944) and musicals--*Fast
and Furious* (with Tim Moore, 1931), and *From Sun to
Sun, a Program of Negro Spirituals and Work Songs*
(1932).
[2, 29, 36, 37, 42]

Imbert, Dennis I.   (New Orleans, LA) novelist

  The Colored Gentlemen. 1931. rpt. New York: AMS
    Press, 1975.

Jamison,   Roscoe   Conkling (1886-1918, Winchester, TN)
poet

  Negro Soldiers and Other Poems. Kansas City, KS:
    Press of the Gray Printing Co, 1918.

(Poems in Kerlin's *Negro Poets* and James Weldon Johnson's *Book of American Negro Poetry*)

Attended Fisk University. Poems published posthumously by a friend.
[34]

Jenkins, Deadrick Franklin (Pontotoc, MS) poet

   It Was Not My World. Los Angeles: Privately Printed, 1942.
   Letters to My Son. Los Angeles: The Deadrick F.Jenkins Publishing Co., 1947.

Johnson, Charles S. (1893-1956, Bristol, VA) sociologist, editor, author

Attended Virginia Union (A.B., 1917; Litt.D., 1928), University of Chicago (Ph.D., 1918); Howard University (L.H.D., 1941). Worked for the Chicago Urban League (1917-1919), Carnegie Foundation (1918), Chicago Commission of Race Relations (1919-1921), National Urban League (1921), editor of *Opportunity* (1923-1928), Swarthmore College (1933-   ), the U.S Army--served in first world war and the League of Nations (1930). Edited *Ebony and Topaz* (1927), a collection of poetry. His nonfiction works include *The Negro in Chicago* (1922), *Race Relations* (1934), *The Collapse of Cotton Tenancy* (1935)--all co-authored; *The Negro in American Civilization* (1930), *Economic Status of the Negro* (1933), *Shadow of the Plantation* (1934), *Preface to Racial Understanding* (1936), *The Negro College Graduate* (1935), *Growing Up in the Black Belt* (1941), *Statistical Atlas of Southern Countries* (1941), *Patterns of Negro Segregation* (1943). Articles published in *Survey Graphic*, *Missionary Review*, *Survey*, and the *American Journal of Sociology*, among others. Honors include the Anisfield Award in 1938 for *The Negro College Graduate*, the William E. Harmon gold medal for distinguished achievement among Negroes in Science (1930).
[13, 36,]

Johnson, Edward Augustus (1860-1944, Raleigh, NC) lawyer, legislator, teacher, alderman, assistant to district attorney

   Light Ahead for the Negro. New York: Grafton Press, 1904.

Early education by a free colored woman, Nancy
Walton, and at Washington High School, Raleigh.
Attended Atlanta University, Shaw University. Taught
in Atlanta and Raleigh, North Carolina, before
studying law at Shaw where he taught for 14 years.
Began his public career as alderman of the city of
Raleigh, then assistant to the District Attorney of
Eastern North Carolina. Began practicing law in
1907. Was the first black man elected to the New York
legislature and was re-elected in 1918. Campaigned
for congress in 1928. Wrote a history book for
colored children in the South even though he was told
that it might cost him his job. Other works include
Adam vs. the Ape Man and Ethiopia.
[*The Crisis* 40 (April 1938): 81-82.]

Johnson, Georgia Douglas (1886-1966, Atlanta, GA)
biographer, playwright, novelist, poet

  The Heart of a Woman, and Other Poems. Boston:
  Cornhill, 1918.
  Bronze. Boston: B.J. Brimmer Co., 1922.
  Blue Blood. Appleton & Co., 1927.
  Plumes: A Play in one act. New York: French,
  1927.
  Share My World. (n.d.)
  An Autumn Cycle. New York: Harold Vinal, LTD,
  1928.

Studied at Atlanta University, Howard University, and
Oberlin Conservatory of Music. Taught school in
Alabama and worked for the government in Washington.
Has published in more than forty anthologies. She is
credited with the publication of one novel, 30 one-
act plays, three books of verse, one biography (*The
Black Cabinet*, 1931), one hundred short stories, six
books of wise sayings, one thousand homely
philosophies, and thirty songs. Contributed to
Opportunity, *Crisis* and other journals and magazines.
[*54, 42, 57*]

Johnson, Helen Aurelia (Hampton, VA) teacher, poet

  A First Harvest. 1932.
  (In Murphy's *Negro Voices*)

Attended Oberlin College, Flora Stone Mather College
of Western Reserve University in Cleveland, Ohio.
Taught at Swift Memorial Junior College in East

Tennessee.   Won   the   Emily   Hills   Poetry   Award   in
1933.   Contributed to *Opportunity*.
[38]

Johnson,   Herbert   Clark   (1911-   ,   Mattoax,   Amelia
County, VA)

  Poems from Flat Creek. 1943.

Attended   school   in   Virginia   and   at   Cheyney   in
Pennsylvania.
[28]

Johnson,   James   Weldon   (1871-1938, Jacksonville, FL)
educator, NAACP officer, novelist, poet

  The Autobiography of an Excoloured Man. 1912. rpt.
   New York, Knopf, 1927.
  Fifty Years. Atlanta: Atlanta University Press,
   1913.
  Fifty Years and Other Poems. Boston: Cornhill,
   1917.
  God's Trombones. New York: Viking, 1927.
  *St. Peter Relates an Incident of the Resurrection
   Day*. New York: Viking Press, 1930.
  Selected Poems.   1936.

Attended   Jacksonville   secondary   schools,   Atlanta
University   (A.M.,   1904),   and   Columbia   University
(graduate   school   for   three   years).   Taught in Henry
County   schools   (Georgia),   Jacksonville   (principal,
Stanton   School,   1894-1901), at Fisk University (1930-
1938)   and   New   York   University   (1934-1937),   and
lectured   at   such schools as Northwestern, University
of   Chicago,   Oberlin   College,   and the University of
North   Carolina.   Admitted   to the Florida Bar in 1897
and   practiced law in Jacksonville. Founded the *Daily
American* newspaper in 1895, edited *New York Age* (1913-
1923).   Served   as   U.S.   Consul   to   Puerto Cabello,
Venzuela   and   Corinto,   Nicaragua (1906-1912). Became
organizer   and   field   secretary   for the NAACP (1916-
1920)   and   executive   secretary   (1920-1930).   Honors
received   include   a Rosenwald fellowship (1929-1930),
the   Spingarn   Medal   (1925), and honorary degrees from
Atlanta   University,   Talladega   College   (1917),   and
Howard University (1923). Publications include   *Self-
determining Haiti* (1920), *The Book of American Negro
Poetry* (1922), *The Book of American Negro Spirituals*
(1925),   *The   Second Book of American Negro Spirituals*
(1926),   *Black   Manhattan* (1930),   his   autobiography

Along This Way (1933), and *Negro Americans, What Now?*
(1934).   His   articles   have   appeared   in   *American*
Mercury,   Forum,   Century,   Harper's   Magazine,   World
Tomorrow, Mento, Southern Workman.
[2, 29, 36, 42]

Jonas, Rosalie (New Orleans, LA) author, poet

  (Contributed to *Crisis* and anthologies)

Jones, Edward Smythe (1881- , Natchez, MS) poet

  The Rose that Bloometh in My Heart and Other Poems
  (by Invincible Ned). Louisville, KY: 1908.
  Souvenir Poem, Our Greater Louisville. Louisville,
  KY: 1908.
  The Sylvan Cabin, A Centenary Ode on the Birth of
  Lincoln and Other Poems. Boston: Sherman French
  and Co., 1911.

Was   given   the opportunity to study at Harvard, after
hearing   of   the University, walking hundreds of miles
from   his home in the South, camping out for the night
and   getting arrested for vagrancy, and gaining public
attention   because   of   the   arrest.   Was given job as
janitor   and   the   opportunity to study during his off
hours.
[56]

Jones,   Joshua   Henry,   Jr.   (1876-   , Orangeburg, SC)
journalist, novelist, poet

  The Heart of the World and Other Poems. Boston:
  Stratford Co., 1919.
  Poems of the Four Seas. Boston, Cornhill, 1921.
  By Sanction of Law. Boston: B.J. Brimmer Co.,
  1924.

Attended Brown University.   Served on the staff of
the   *Providence News* and other New England newspapers,
Boston Advertiser (city   editor).   Also,   served as
secretary   to   Mayor   James   Curley   of   Boston   who
appointed him editor of the *City Record.*
[34]

Jones,   J. McHenry (worked   in   Charleston,   W   VA)
novelist

  Hearts of Gold. 1896. rpt. College Park, MD:
  McGrath, 1969.

Kinds, Levander (1916-1974, Cleveland OH, but worked in MS) dean, junior college president, professor, minister, novelist

> *Reflections*. Cleveland: Central Publishing House, 1946.

Attended Western Reserve University (B.A., 1944; M.A., 1945). Taught philosophy at Leland College (1946-1947); served as Dean of Men at Tougaloo College (1947-1951) and Natchez Junior College (1951-1964), president of Natchez Junior College (1964-1968), and professor at Alcorn State University (1968-1974). Co-edited the *Natchez Times*. Published articles in music and educational journals. Directed a radio broadcast in Vicksburg, Mississippi. Pastored in Mississippi.
[34]

Killens, John Oliver (1916- , Macon, GA) novelist

> *Youngblood*. 1954. rpt. New York: Trident Press, Affiliated Publishers, 1966.

Attended public schools in Macon, Georgia. Worked with the National Labor Relations Board; served with the U.S. Amphibian forces in the U.S. Pacific. Published *And Then We Heard the Thunder* (1964), *Black Man's Burden* (1965), *'Sippi* (1967), *Slaves* (1969), *The Cotillion or One Good Bull Is Half the Herd* (1971), *and Great Gittin' Up Morning: The Adventures of John Henry* (1975). Wrote plays--*Ballad of the Winter Soldiers* (1964), *Lower Than the Angels* (1965), and *Cotillion* (1975,) and screenplays--*Odds Against Tomorrow* (1960), and *Slaves* (1969).
[2, 23, 42]

Laine, Henry Allen (1869-, College Hill, Madison County, KY) teacher, poet

> *Footprints*. Richmond, KY: Cut Rate Publishing Co., 1914.

Educated in the public schools of College Hill, Kentucky and Berea College. Taught at the district school in Brassfield, Kentucky.
[52]

Lane, James Franklin (1874- , Jackson, TN) college president, poet

My Second Trip Abroad. (n.d.)
Much in Little. (n.d.)

Educated at Lane College High School (graduate of normal course) and Walden College (A.B., 1895, A.M., Ph.D., 1903). Principal in Sardis Mississippi; teacher, department chairman and president of Lane College.
[57]

Lanusse, Armand (1812-1869, New Orleans, LA) soldier, author, educator, poet

Educated in New Orleans. First elected principal of Bernard Convent Institute for Indigent Catholic Orphans (1852-1866). Contributed columns to *L'Union* and *La Tribune* of New Orleans, and to *L'Album Litteraire.* Edited *Les Cenelles,* an anthology of poetry by creoles of color (1845).
[14, 36,]

Lee, George Washington (1894- , Indianola, MS) novelist

   Beale Street Sundown. New York: House of Field, 1942.
   River George. New York: The McCauley Company, 1937.

Attended Alcorn A&M in Lorman, Mississippi. Served as vice president for Mississippi Life Insurance Company (1922-1924).
[11]

Lee, John Francis (1873- , Alexandria, VA) clergyman, editor, poet

   Poems. Norfolk: Burke and Gregory Print, 1905.
   What Ye Gone'do Wif Ham. (n.d.)
   Discords and Harmony. (n.d.)
   The Prince of Ebony. 1907

Educated at Livingstone College in Salisbury, North Carolina (A.B., A.M.), Gammon School of Theology, Boston University, American School of Law in Chicago (graduate), and Northwestern University (postgraduate work). Editor of Sunday School materials of the African Methodist Episcopal Zion Church.
[57]

Lipscomb, Edward Hart (1858- , Orange County, Durham, NC) Baptist minister, educator, editor, college president, poet

Attended school in Raleigh, North Carolina, Shaw Collegiate Institute (B.A., 1879). Helped to found the *African Expositor*. Taught at Shaw University (1879-1881, 1883-1884); editor of the *Baptist Standard*; principal of Durham graded school (1881-1883), Dallas Academy in North Carolina--president when it became Western Union Institute.
[52, 53]

Love, Ruth Leary (NC) teacher, poet

  Nebraska and His Granny. Tuskegee, AL: Tuskegee
    Institute Press, 1931.

Attended Barber-Scotia and Johnson C. Smith. Taught school in North Carolina. Published *A Collection of Folklore for Children*.
[15]

Lyles, Aubrey (1884-1932, Jackson, TN) teacher, comedian, actor, lyricist, playwright

  Lazy Rhythm (n.d.)
  Darkydom, 1914-1915
  Running Wild, 1923
  Rang Tang, 1927
  Keep Shuffling, 1928

Attended Fisk University.
[37]

Madgett, Naomi Long (1923- , Norfolk, VA) educator, poet

  Songs to a Phantom Nightingale. New York:
    Fortuny's Publishers, 1941.

Attended Virginia State College (B.A., 1945), Wayne State University (M.A., 1956), University of Detroit, and Wayne State University. Taught in Detroit (1955-1968) East Michigan University (1968-). Served as associate editor of Lotus Press (1974-). Worked as a reporter for various newspapers. Other works include *One and the Many* (1956), *Star by Star* (1965), *Pink Ladies in the Afternoon* (1972), *Exits and Entrances* (1978), *Phantom Nightingale* (1981),

Success in Language and Literature (1967), and *A Student's Guide to Creative Writing* (1980).
[1, 42]

Major, Clarence (1936–   Atlanta, GA) essayist, anthologist, editor, lexicographer, poet, novelist

  The Fires that Burn in Heaven. Chicago: 1954.
  [23]

Majors, Monroe Alpheus (1864– , born in Waco, TX, but attended schools in the South) physician, author, lecturer, editor, civil rights leader, poet

  Ode to Frederick Douglas. 1917.
  First Steps to Nursery Rhymes. 1921.
  (Poems also published in the *Washington Bee*, the *Peoples Advocate*, and other newspapers.)

Educated at Tillotson College and Normal (1881-83); Central Tennessee State College (1883-86); Meharry Medical College (M.D., 1883-86). Practiced medicine in Texas--Brenham, Calvert, and Dallas; was the first black to pass the California Board of Examiners (1889); practiced medicine in Waco, Texas (1890-1895, 1899-1901) opening a drugstore there, in Decatur, Illinois (1895-1899), in Chicago 1901-1923) and in California until about 1955. Edited the *Texas Searchlight* (1893-1895), *The Indianapolis Freeman* (associate editor, 1898-1899), the *Chicago Broad Ax* , and the *Chicago Conservator* (1908).
[57]

Martin, John Sella (1832-1900, NC) poet

  (Poetry in *Anglo-African Magazine*, I (1859), 361-62)

Baptist minister, lecturer, editor of *New Era* (Washington, D.C.)
[52]

Matheus, John Frederick (1887-1983, Keyser, W VA) poet, historian, teacher

  (Short stories in *Opportunity*--May 1925, July 1926, April 1926, October 1926, October 1927, August 1928, December 1929, July 1931; *Crisis*--December 1926, November 1931; *The Carolina Magazine*--May 1928, April 1929; *Poet Lore*--September 1930.

Poetry, short stories, and plays in such anthologies as *The Negro* (Locke, 1925), *Plays of Negro Life* (Locke and Gregory, 1927), *Caroling Dust* (Cullen), *An Anthology of American Negro Literature* (Calverton, 1929), *Plays and Pageants of the Life of the Negro* (Richardson, 1930), *Ebony and Topaz* (Johnson), *Readings from Negro Authors* (Cromwell, Turner, Dykes, 1931), *The Negro Caravan* (Brown, 1941). Some poems in *Opportunity*, *Crisis*, *The Chronicle*, *Carolina Magazine*, and *Negro Digest*.)

Early schooling in Steubenville, Ohio; attended Adelbert College of Western Reserve University (A.B., 1910), Columbia University (M.A., 1921), and the University of Paris. Worked at Florida A&M University (1910-1922), West Virginia Collegiate Institute (1922-1952); in Liberia in 1930 as secretary to Charles S. Johnson, head of the National Urban League, and as Director of the teaching of English in the national schools of the Republic of Haiti (1945-1946). Held the office of treasurer of the College Language Association for 32 years. Decorated as "Officier de l'Ordre Nationale Honneur et Merite by the Haitian government for his literary efforts, radio broadcasts in Port-au-Prince, and his interest and support of Haiti. Awarded first prize in *Opportunity*'s 1925 literary contest for the short story, "Fog," and first prize in the 1926 *Crisis* literary contest for the short story, "Swamp Moccasin." Wrote a number of plays that appeared in several anthologies, and a book of short stories.
[6, 17, 42]

Mayfield, Julian (1928- , Greer, SC) playwright, novelist
  Fire, 1949
  The Other Foot, 1952
  World Full of Men, 1952

Studied at Lincoln University in Pennsylvania, Paul Mann Actors Workshop. Worked mostly as playwright, director, and actor. Edited newspaper for Guyanna government. Publications after 1953: *The Hit* (1957), *The Long Night* (1958), and *The Grand Parade* (1961).
[37, 41]

Means, Sterling M., poet

  The Black Devils and Other Poems. Louisville, KY:
    Pentacostal Publishing, 1919.

   The Deserted Cabin and Other Poems.   Atlanta: A.B.
   Caldwell Co., 1915.
[34]

Menard, John Willis (1838-1893, born in Kakaskia, IL
but   worked   in   the   South)   congressman,   state
representative,   customs   inspector   and   street
commissioner, editor, postal clerk, justice of the
peace, a deputy collector of internal revenue, poet

   Lays in Summer Lands. Washington: Enterprise
   Publishing Co., 1879)

Attended   school   in   Sparta,   Illinois   and   Iberia
College   in   Ohio.   Appointed a clerk in the Bureau of
Emigration,   becoming   the   first black federal clerk.
Worked   as a customs inspector and street commissioner
(1865-1871).   Elected   the   first black congressman in
1868 but never served.   Served a term in the Florida
legislature.   Selected as a delegate to the Republican
National   Convention   in   1876. Published a newspaper,
The   Free   South (later the *Radical Standard*); edited
and   published   the   *Florida   Sun* (Jacksonville), and
edited   the   *Key   West   News*   and   the *Southern Leader*
(Jacksonville).
[52]

Miller,   Clifford   L.   (Columbia,   TN)   columnist,
writer, minister, poet

   Haunting Voice.   Lavalle, 1924.
   Wings Over Dark Waters: A Poetic Drama.   NY:
   Great Concord Publishers, 1954.

Graduate   of   Fisk   University   (B.A.,   1904), Andover
Theological   Seminary   (B.D.,   1907),   Fisk University
(M.A.,   1918).   Columnist   for   the   *Boston Guardian,
Fisk   News,   Boston   Chronicle,* and the *Amsterdam News*
of   New   York   City;   radio speaker on "Your Brother's
Voice,"   a   race   relations   program.   Minister   in
Massachusetts,   France   (army chaplain), Alabama, Rhode
Island, and New York.
[57, Introduction to *Wings Over Dark Waters*]

Miller,   Flournoy   (1887-1971,   Nashville,   TN)
actor/composer, playwright

   The Oyster Man (with Aubrey Lyles, and Hal Reid,
   1907)
   Shuffle Along (with Lyles, 1921)

Running Wild (with Lyles, 1923)
Brownskin Models (with Lyles, 1927)
Keep Shufflin' (with Lyles, 1928)
Blackbirds of 1930 (with A. Razaf)
Lazy Rhythm (with Razaf, 1931)
Shuffle Along of 1933 (with Noble Sissle, 1932)
Meet Miss Jones (with J.J. Johnson, 1947)

Attended Fisk University.
[37]

Miller, May (Washington, D.C.) editor, teacher, dramatist

Negro History in Thirteen Plays. Washington,
   D.C.: Associated, 1935. (with Willis Richardson)

Attended Howard University, with advanced work at American University and Columbia University. Taught speech and drama at Frederick Douglass High School in Baltimore; worked at Monmouth College in Illinois as lecturer and poet-in-residence. Published after 1954: *Into the Clearing*, 1959; and *Poems*, 1962; *Lyrics of Three Women*, 1964; *Not That Far*, 1973; *The Clearing and Beyond*, 1974; *Dust of Uncertain Journey*, 1975.)
[37, 42]

Mitchell, Loften (1919- , born in New York, but attended school in the South)

The Cellar (1947)

Attended De Witt Clinton High School, City College of New York, Talladega College College (B.A., 1943), and Columbia University. Worked as social investigator, script writer for stage, television and radio. Edited NAACP *Freedom Journal*. Awarded Guggenheim Foundation Award for Creative Writing (1958-1959). Has written a number of plays and screenplays, including *Investigation Report* (1959), *Tell Pharaoh* (1963), *Ballad for Bimshire* (with Irving Burgie, 1963), *Land Beyond the River; A Play in Three Acts* (1963), *Ballad of the Winter Soldiers* (with John O. Killens, 1964), *Star of the Morning* (1965), *The Stubborn Old Lady Who Resisted Change* (1973), and *Voices of the Black Theater* (1975). Nonfiction includes *Black Drama; The Story of the American Negro in the Theatre* (1967).
[37, 42]

Morrison, William Lorenzo (lived in Washington, D.C.)
poet

   Dark Rhapsody. New York: H. Harrison, 1945.

Graduate of Bluefield College in West Virginia.

Morse,   Leonard   Francis   (1891- , worked in FL)
educator, clergyman, poet

   Dawn of Tomorrow. Gulf City Publishing
     Co., 1923.

Attended   Howard   University   (A.B.,   1915),   Payne
University   Divinity   School   (D.D.,   1920),
Northwestern Louisiana (A.M., 1930).
[57]

Morton, Lena B., poet, anthologist

Nonfiction writings include *Negro Poetry in America*
(1925) and *My First Sixty Years: Passion for Wisdom*
(poems interspersed, 1965).

Murphy, Beatrice (1908- , born in Monesson, PA but
lived in Washington, D.C.) teacher, anthologist, poet

   Love is Terrible Thing. New York: Hobson Book
     Press, 1945. (poems)
   (Poems in anthologies such as *The Parnassian*, 1930,
   Contemporary American Women Poets, 1938, *The Light
   of Day*, 1929, *Crown Anthology of Verse* , 1938, and
   her own *Negro Voices*, 1938; and in journals and
   magazines)

Graduated from Dunbar High School (Washington, D.C.)
in 1928.   Conducted a column for the *Washington
Tribune* called "Think It Over" (1933-1935); feature
editor and children's page editor for the same paper
(1935-1937); book review editor of the *Afro American*
(1938-).   Worked as secretary to the head of the
Sociology Department at the Catholic University of
America and as stenographer in the U.S. Office of
Price Administration; also, operated a circulating
library and a public stenography shop.   Two
anthologies: *Ebony Rhythm* and *Negro Voices*. Two
works after 1954: *The Rocks Cry Out* (1969) and
Today's Negro Voices (1970).

McBrown, Gertrude Parthenia (Charleston, SC) playwright, poet

  The Picture Poetry Book. Washington, D.C.:
   Associated, 1935.
[16]

McCall, James Edward (1880- , Montgomery, AL) poet, short story writer

  (Contributed poetry to anthologies, a number of Southern daily newspapers, and the *New York World*)

Early education in the public schools of Montogomery; graduate of Alabama State Normal (B.S., 1900); Howard University (attended medical school until typhoid fever rendered him blind); attended Albion College in Michigan (M.S., 1905). Publisher of *The Emancipator*, a Montgomery race weekly; city editor and editorial writer for the *Detroit Independent*.
[44]

McCarthy, Eugene V. (New Orleans) physician, poet

  (In *La Tribune*)

Educated in France. Practiced medicine in New Orleans.

McClellan, George Marion (1860-1934, Belfast, TN) financial agent, principal, theologian, poet, short story writer

  Poems and Storiettes. Nashville: The Author, 1895.
   Songs of a South. Boston: Press of Rockwell and Churchell, 1896.
   Old Greenbottom Inn and Other Stories. Louisville, KY: The Author, 1906.
   The Path of Dreams. Louisville, KY: Morton, 1916.
   (In James W. Johnson's *The Book of American Negro Poetry*)

Educated at Fisk University and at Hartford Theological Seminary. Worked as financial agent for Fisk University and as principal of Paul Laurence Dunbar School in Louisville.
[32]

McGirt, James Ephraim (1874-1930, Robeson, NC) editor, publisher, realtor, poet

Avenging the Maine. Raleigh, NC: Edwards and
  Broughton Printers and Binders, 1899.
*Some Simple Songs and a Few More Ambitious
  Attempts*. Philadephia: George F. Lasher Printers
  and Binders, 1901.
The Triumphs of Ephraim (novel). Philadephia: The
  McGirt Publishing Co., 1907.
For Your Sweet Sake; Poems. Philadephia: The John
  C. Winston Company, 1909.

Attended school in Lumberton, North Carolina,
Greensboro public schools; Bennett College (B.A.,
1895). Edited and published *McGirt's Magazine*, and
worked as ghost writer for the *North Carolina
Review*. Manager of the Hair Grower Manufacturing
Company; realtor.
[3, 36]

Nash, Theodore Edward Delafayette (1881-   ,
Portsmouth, VA) insurance company superintendent,
novelist

  Love and Vengeance, or Viola's Victory.
    Portsmouth, VA: Privately printed, 1903.

Educated at Chestnutt Street High School in
Portsmouth, Virginia. Worked as insurance company
superintendent for Beneficial Insurance for 20 years,
and as director and treasurer the Tidewater Building.
[57]

Nelson, Alice Ruth Moore Dunbar (1875-1935, New
Orleans, LA) teacher, social worker, editor, writer

  Violets and Other Tales. Boston: Monthly Review
    Publishing, 1895.
  The Goodness of St. Roque and Other Stories.
    1899. rpt. College Park, MD: McGrath, 1969.

Attended Straight College in New Orleans, the
University of Pennsylvania, Cornell University, and
the School of Industrial Arts in Philadephia,
Pennsylvania. Taught school in New Orleans and New
York. Nonfiction works include *Masterpieces of Negro
Eloquence* (1914) and *Romances of the Negro in
American History*.
[52, 57]

Newsome, Mary Effie Lee (1885- , born in Philadephia,
PA, but lived in the Alabama) writer

Our Young People's Book of Verse. Roberts and
  Sons, 1923.
Gladiola Gardens. Washington, D.C.: Associated,
  1940.
(Poems in *Crisis, Black World, Opportunity,* and *St.
Nicholas*)

Attended Wilberforce University (1901-1904), Oberlin
(1904-1905), the Academy of Fine Arts (1907-1908),
and the University of Pennsylvania (1911-1914).
Edited the "Little Page" in *Crisis.*
[17]

Pawley, Thomas D., Jr. (1917- , Jackson, MS)
dramatist

  Jedgement Day, 1938
  Smokey, 1938
  Freedom in My Soul, 1938
  Son of Liberty, 1938

Attended Virginia State College and the University of
Iowa. Worked as director of dramatics at Prairie
View, Lincoln University, and Atlanta University
(Summer Theatre).
[11, 37]

Payne, Daniel A. (1811-1893, Charleston, SC) bishop,
editor, poet

  Pleasures and Other Miscellaneous Poems.
    Baltimore, MD: Sherwood and Co., 1850.

Attended school supported by the Minor's Society;
received private instruction. Learned shoemaking,
carpentry, and tailoring. Attended the Lutheran
Seminary in Gettysburg, Pennsylvania. Received
LL.D. from Lincoln University in 1880 and the D.D.
from Wilberforce University. Taught in Charleston
and also in Philadephia. Ordained bishop of the
A.M.E. Church in 1852. Purchased Wilberforce
University for the A.M.E. Church and was president of
the school 1863-1876, the first Negro college
president in the western world. Editor-in-Chief,
*Repository of Religion and of Literature and Science
and Art* (1858-1863).
[42, 53]

Pickens, William (1881-1954, Anderson County, SC)
educator, orator, editor, and civil rights leader

*The Vengeance of Gods and Three Other Stories of
_Real American Color Line Life.* Philadelphia:
A.M.E. Book Concern, 1922.
Bursting Bonds. (n.d.)
American Aesop, Negro and Other Humor. Boston:
Jordan and Moore Press, 1926.

Attended Little Rock High School, Arkansas; Talladega
college before transferring to Yale (B.A., 1904).
Taught at Talladega (1904-1914), Wiley University in
Marshall, Texas (1914-1915), Morgan College in
Baltimore, Maryland (1915-1920). Served as Field
Secretary for the NAACP (1920-1940). Took leave from
NAACP duties in 1937, to lecture for the Federal
Forum Project, and in 1941, to serve as director of
the Interracial Section of the Treasury Department's
Savings Bonds Division. Was an active civil rights
leader. Contributed to Associated Negro Press.
[36]

Pitts, Richard (1910-   , two miles east of
Mashuville, MS--Noxubee County) poet

  Excelsior, Book of Poems. Holly Springs, MS:
   Privately Printed, 1944.

Attended Rust College in Holly Springs, Mississippi.
[Introduction to *Excelsior*]

Poston, Theodore (1906-1974, Hopkinsville, KY)
journalist and short story writer

  (Contributed to O'Brien's *Best Short Stories, Negro
  Caravan, Crisis, Phylon, The Nation, Scribner's,
  Opportunity, New Republic*)

Educated in Hopkinsville, Kentucky, Tennessee State
College (A.B., 1928), and New York University
(graduate work). Was managing editor of *New York
Contender*; editor, *Pittsburgh Courier*; City Editor,
New York-Amsterdam Star News; feature writer and
reporter, *New York Post*. Also, served as public
relations consultant, Chief of Negro News Desk,
Office of War Information (1940-).
[27]

Powell, Adam Clayton, Sr. (1865-1953, Franklin
County, VA) clergyman, novelist

Picketing Hell. New York: Wendell Maliett Co., 1942.

Attended Wayland Academy-Virginia Union University (1892), Virginia Union University (D.D., 1904), Virginia Seminary and College (D.D., 1904), Howard University (D.D., 1924), and Yale University Divinity School. Pastored in New Haven, Connecticut (1893-1908) and in New York City (1908-1937). Honors include the Harmon Award (1928). Nonfiction: *Patriotism and the Negro* (1918), *Against the Tide, an Autobiography* (1938, 1980), *Palestine and Saints in Caesar's Household* (1939), *Riots and Ruins* (1945), *Upon this Rock: the History of the Abyssinian Baptist Church* (1949).
[42]

Ragland, J. Farley (1904- , South Boston, VA) pharmacist-drugstore owner, journalist, minister

Lyrics and Laughter. Lawrenceville, VA: The Brunswick Times Gazette Press, 1939.
The Hometown Sketchbook. Lawrenceville, VA: The Brunswick Times Gazette Press, 1940.
Rhymes of the Times. New York: W. Malliett and Co., 1946.

Attended Virginia State College, Hampton Institute and Howard University. Proprietor of Campus Pharmacy in Lawrenceville, Virginia. Wrote the theme song for the National Negro Exposition in Chicago, 1940. Works appear in a number of anthologies and journals.
[57]

Razafenkeriefo, Andre*amenentaia*, "Andy Razaf" (1895-1973, Washington, D.C.) poet and songwriter

Hot Chocolates, 1929
Blackbirds of 1930 (with Flournoy Miller, 1930)
Lazy Rhythm (with Flournoy Miller, 1931)
(Regular contributor to *The Crusader*, and *The Negro World*; anthologized in Kerlin's *Negro Poets and Their Poems*)

Attended public school. Received the U.S. Department Silver Medal (1946) and was inducted into the Songwriters Hall of Fame (1972). Wrote many musical compositions.
[34, 37]

Reason, Arthur W.   (Leesburg, FL) poet, teacher

(Poems in *World's Fair Anthology*, *America Speaks*, *Songs and Lyrics*, *United We Sing*, *Sing, Laugh, Weep*)

Educated in the public school of Leesburg, Florida, Oberlin Academy, Oberlin College, Teachers College at Howard University (B.S., 1913), the University of Nebraska, and the University of Wisconsin (postgraduate work). Served as principal of schools in Oklahoma and Missouri. One of the organizers of The Scribes, a club devoted to encouraging people to write and appreciate poetry.
[24, 51]

Redding, J. Saunders (1906- , Wilmington, DL) professor, critic, novelist

Strangers and Alone. New York: Harcourt, Brace, 1950.

Attended Brown University (A.B., 1928; M.A., 1932) and Columbia University. Taught at State Teachers College, Elizabeth City, North Carolina; Hampton Institute, Hampton, Virginia; Louisville Municipal College; Morehouse; and Cornell University. Received the Rosenwald Foundation Fellowship (1940). Articles published in *North American Review*, *Transition*, *Harper's Magazine*, *American Mercury*, and *Atlantic Monthly*. Nonfiction works include *To Make a Poet Black* (1939), *No Day of Triumph* (1942), *They Came in Chains: Americans from Africa* (1950), *On Being a Negro in America* (1951), *The Lonesome Road* (1958), *The Negro* (1967). Awarded at least six honorary degrees.
[22, 42]

Richardson, Willis (1889- , Wilmington, NC) dramatist

Plays and Pageants from the Life of the Negro. Washington, D.C.: Associated, 1930.
Negro History in Thirteen Plays.   Washington, D.C.: Associated, 1935.
(Plays in *Carolina Magazine*, *Crisis*, and in anthologies including Alain Locke's *The New Negro*)

Attended public schools of Washington, D.C.; correspondence course in poetry and drama (1916-

1918). Dramatist, (U.S. Government clerk and mechanic while pursuing playwright career). Was the first black playwright to have a play produced on Broadway (*The Chip Woman's Fortune*, 1923). His plays have been performed by the Krigwa Players, a group formed by W.E.B. Dubois (*The Flight of the Natives*, 1927), the Howard Players directed by Montgomery George and Alain Locke, the Dunbar Players (*Mortgaged*, 1923, 1924), the Raymond O'Neil's Ethiopian Players in Chicago, Washington and on Broadway (1922-1923). Awards include the Amy Spingarn prize for *The Broken Banjo* (*Crisis*, 1925) and for *Bootblack Lover* (1926); and the Edith Fisher Schwab Cup at Yale University Theatre. His articles/essays were published in journals/magazines such as *Crisis* and *Opportunity*.
[42, 37, 57].

Ridout, Daniel Lyman (poet)

   Verses from a Humble Cottage. Hampton, VA:
   Hampton Institute Press, 1924.

Worked at Princess Ann Academy, Princess Anne, Maryland.
[Introduction to Verses]

Rillieux, Victor-Ernest (1842-1898, New Orleans, LA) poet
   Les Feuilles Mortes. New Orleans: The Daily
   Crusader, 1895.

Conducted a small establishment, but spent much of his time writing. Some poems published in various magazines and newspapers, other set to music.
[48]

Rogers, Alex (1876- , Nashville, TN) poet, playwright

   Abyssinia (with J.A. Shipp, 1906)
   Bandanna Land (with J.A. Shipp, 1908)
   In Dahomey (with J.A. Shipp and Paul Laurence
   Dunbar, 1902)
   Lode of Koal (with J.A. Shipp and Bert Williams,
   1909)
   The Traitor (with Henry Creamer, 1912)
   The Old Man's Boy (with Henry Creamer, 1914)
   Dark Town Follies (with Leubrie Hill, 1913)
   This and That, 1919
   Baby Blues, 1919

Charlie (Harry Cort, 1923)
Go-Go (Harry Cort, George Stoddard, 1923)
My Magnolia (with Eddie Hunter, 1926)
(In *Singers in the Dawn*)
[12]

Rowe, George C. (1853-1903, born in Litchfield, Connecticut, but worked in VA, GA, and SC) minister, editor, author, poet

Sunbeams. Hampton, 1880--no copy found.
Thoughts in Verse and a Volume of Poems. Charleston: SC: Kahrs, Stolze and Welch, 1887.
Our Heroes: Patriotic Poems on Men, Women, and Sayings of the Negro Race. Charleston, SC: Author, 1890.
Decoration (poem). 1891

Early schooling in Litchfield, Connecticut. Certificate of trade after apprenticeship on the *Litchfield Enquirer.* Worked in the Normal School printing office, Hampton, Virginia. Edited and published the *Charleston Enquirer,* 1893-1896. Pastor in McIntosh, Georgia (1881-1885) and in Charleston, South Carolina (1885-1897). Memorial Souvenir verse tributes (1890, 1894, 1903) and *The Aim of Life,* an address (1892) were also published.

Sejour, Victor (1817-1874, New Orleans, LA) playwright/dramatist

(In *Rives des Coloreis,* 1837)

Lived in Paris from age 17. Was instructed by Michel Selizay in St. Barke Academy.
[14, 36, 48]

Shackleford, Otis M. (1871-) novelist

Seeking the Best. Kansas City, MO: Franklin Hudson Publishing Co., 1909.
Lillian Simmons. Kansas City, MO: Burton, 1915.

Shackleford, William H. (1878- Selma, AL) proprietor, manufacturer, poet, novelist

Pearls in Prose and Poetry. Nashville: National Baptist Publishing Board, 1907.
Poems. Nashville: AMESSU Press, 1915.
Along the Highway (fiction). Nashville: AMESSU, 1916.

Proprietor of a beauty shop; manufacturer of toilet specialties.
[57]

Shaw, O'Wendell

  Greater Need Below. Columbus: Bi-Monthly Negro
  Book Club, 1936.

Shine, Ted (1936- , Baton Rouge, LA) teacher, playwright

  Cold Day in August, 1950
  Sho' Is Hot in the Cotton Patch, 1951

Attended public school in Dallas; college at Howard University (B.A., 1953), University of Iowa, and the University of California. Taught at several colleges, including Howard University, Dillard University, and Prairie View College. Wrote a number of plays that have been performed since 1953 including *Epitaph for a Bluebird* (1958), *Morning, Noon and Night* (1965), *Contribution* (1969), *Shoes* (1969), *Comback, After the Fire* (1969), *Flora's Kisses* (1969), *Three One Act Plays* (1970), and *Plantation* (1970).
[42]

Silvera, Edward Samuel (1906-1937, Jacksonville, FL) poet

  (In *Sing, Laugh, Weep*)

Graduated from Orange High School.

Smith, Lucy (1888-1955, Wilmington, NC) poet, educator

  No Middle Ground.

Attended public school in Pennsylvania.
[57]

Smith, S.P. (Fayetteville, NC) poet

  Our Alma Mater and Other Poems. Washington, D.C.:
  copyright by Rev. A.C. Garner, 1904.

Spencer, Anne (1882-1975, Bramwell, VA) social worker, librarian

(Poems in Johnson's *The Book of the American Negro Poetry*, Locke's *The New Negro*, Cullen's *Caroling Dusk*, and Johnson's *Ebony and Topaz*)

Educated at Virginia Seminary in Lynchburg; social worker and librarian.
[11]

Stowers, Walter H. (1859-   , Owensboro, KY) lawyer, county supervisor, novelist

  Appointed. 1894. rpt. New York: AMS Press, 1970.
  (William H. Anderson (psuedonym: Sana)

Attended Detroit High school, Mayhew Business University, and Detroit College of Law. Served as supervisor of Wayne County, Michigan.
[57]

Tarry, Ellen (1906-   , Birmingham, AL) teacher, feature writer, writer of juvenile literature

  Janie Belle. New York: Garden City Publishers, 1940.
  Hezekiah Horton. New York: Viking Press, 1942.
  _____and Marie H.E. Ets. *My Dog Rinty*. New
  York: Viking, 1946.
  The Runaway Elephant. New York: Viking, 1950.

Attended Slater Public High School in Birmingham; St. Francis De Sales School, Rock Castle, Virginia; and Alabama State Teachers College. Studied in New York in the Writers' Laboratory, Bureau of Educational Experiments. Taught grammar school. Worked as a feature writer for *Alabama Truth*, a Negro weekly, and the *Amsterdam News* (New York); associate director of the Chicago Friendship House, and assistant director of the USO Club in Anniston, Alabama. Articles published in *Catholic World, Catholic Digest, The Eikon* (Canada).
[50]

Thierry, Camille (1814-1875, New Orleans, LA) poet

  (In *Les Cenelles* and in *La Chronique* and *L'Orleanis*)

Left New Orleans to live abroad.
[48]

Thomas, David Gatewood (Norfolk, VA) business manager, poet

The Voice from the Wilderness. (n.d.)

Served as organizer and president of the State Federation of Male Glee Clubs in Virginia; business manager of the Philaharmonic Glee Club of Norfolk, Virginia.
[38]

Thomas, Joseph Turner (1874- , Greenville, AL) physician

A Plea for the Congo State. 1909.

Attended Pensacola High School and A&M College in Alabama (1896); Meharry College (M.D., 1905). Practiced medicine; songwriter. Founded Lincoln Hospital in Cleveland.
[57]

Thompson, Eloise A. *Bibb* (See Bibb, Eloise A.)

Tinsley, Tomi Carolyn, poet

_____Lucia M. Pitts and Helen C. Harris. *Triad.*
  Washington, D.C.: Privately printed, 1945.
  (Freelance, published in magazines and newspapers.)

Graduate of Virginia State College; professor at North Carolina College, Durham, North Carolina.
[38]

Todd, Walter E. (Washington, D.C.) novelist

Fireside Musings. Washington, D.C.: Murray Bros.,
  1909.
Gathered Treasures. Washington, D.C.: Murray
  Bros., 1912.
A Little Sunshine. Washington, D.C.: Murray
  Bros., 1917.
Parson Johnson's Lecture. Washington, D.C.:
  Murray Bros., 1906.
Young Men's Christian Association (a poem).
  Washington, D.C.: Oscar D. Morris Printer, 1905.

Tolson, Melvin (1900-1966, Moberly, MO, but attended school in TN) professor, poet

Rendezvous with America. New York: Dodd, Mead, and Co., 1944.
Libretto for the Republic of Liberia. New York: Twayne, 1953.

Studied at Fisk, Lincoln and Columbia Universities. Taught briefly at several Southern colleges before going to Langston where he was director of the University's Dust Bowl Theatre and professor of creative literature. Published *Harlem Gallery* in 1965.
[11, 42]

Toomer, [Nathan] Jean (1894-1967, Washington, D.C.) dramatist, poet, author

Cane. New York: Boni and Liverwright, 1923.

Attended Dunbar High School in Washington, D.C., University of Wisconsin, and for short periods-- Massachusetts College for Agriculture, and physical-training college in Chicago; studied at Gurdjieff Institute in Fontainbleau (1924). Sold cars in Chicago, taught physical education in Milwaukee and worked as a shipfitter in New Jersey during WWI. Principal in Sparta, Georgia (1921), and taught school in Pennsylvania after WWI. Poems published in *The Double Dealer, Broom, The Dial, Opportunity, Crisis, Little Review.*
[36,42]

Tracy, Robert A. (1878- , practiced medicine in GA) novelist

The Sword of Nemesis. New York: The Neal Publishing Co., 1919.

Troup, Cornelius V., Sr. (1902- , Brunswick, GA) educator, poet

(In *Negro Voices, Music Unheard, Badge of Honor, and Ebony Rhythm*)

Attended in Brunswick, Georgia public school, Morris Brown (B.S., 1925), Atlanta University (M.S., 1937), the University of Minnesota, and Ohio State University (Ph.D., 1947). Was principal of high schools in Decatur and Brunswick, Georgia. Served as registrar of Fort Valley State College (1945-). Awarded honorary degrees from Wilberforce University

(LL.D., 1949) and Morris Brown (LL.D., 1959).
Published *Distinguished Negro Georgians* in 1962.
[54]

Turner, Rev. Henry McNeal (1833-1915, Newberry Court
House, SC) bishop of the AME Church, U.S. Chaplain,
orator, poet

Informal schooling under benevolent white woman and
various ministers and professors. Attended
Wilberforce (D.D., 1873); received Honorary L.L.D.
from Pennsylvania University (1872). Was appointed
U.S. Chaplain to colored troops by President Lincoln
in 1863. Bishop in Georgia, Alabama, Tennessee.
[8, 53]

Turpin, Waters E. (1910-1968, Oxford, Eastern Shore,
MD) professor, novelist

  These Low Grounds. New York: Harper, 1937.
  O Canaan. New York: Doubleday, Doran, 1939.
  The Rootless. New York: Vantage, 1957.

Attended Morgan College (B.A.) and Columbia
University (M.A., Ph.D.). Taught at Storer College
(Harper's Ferry, Virginia) and Lincoln University.
Received the Rosenwald Fellowship for creative
writing to write *The Rootless.*
[11, 42]

Tyler, Ephrain David (Grand Cane, LA) poet

  Tyler's Poems. Shreveport, LA: The Author, n.p.

Attended public school, entered Colsman Academy,
Gibsland, Louisiana; finished manual training at
Tuskegee Institute. Taught manual training in
Mississippi for two years, then became a fulltime
poet. Called the Poet Laureate of Louisiana.

Vashon, George B. (1824-1878, spent time in MS and
Washington, D.C.) poet

Attended Oberlin College (A.B., 1844; M.A., 1849).
Taught at New York Central College, College Faustin
(Port-au-Prince, Haiti). Admitted to the New York
Bar in 1847; practiced in Syracuse, New York before
becoming Dean of the Howard University Law School.
Left Howard to go to Mississippi where he died during

a yellow fever epidemic in Rodney, Mississippi.
Poems in anthologies.
[6]

Walden, Islay (1847-1884, Randolph County, NC) poet

  Miscellaneous Poems. Washington: Author, 1873.
  Walden's Miscellaneous Poems, Which the Author
   Desires to Dedicate to the Cause of Education and
   Humanity. Washington D.C.: Reid and Woodward,
   Printers, 1872.
  Walden's Sacred Poems, with a Sketch of His Life.
   News Brunswick, N.J.: Terhune and Van Auglen's
   Press, 1877.

Graduated from Howard Normal School and attended New
Brunswick   Theological   Seminary   (ordained   and
licensed).   Worked in the mines of North Carolina
while a slave and before going to Washington, D.C.
for medical attention and to attend school. Did
manual labor and sold his poetry on the streets of
Washington, D.C.. Lectured in Pennsylvania and New
Jersey before settling in New Brunswick to sell his
poetry for awhile.   Served as minister in North
Carolina.
[46, 52]

Walker, Margaret Abigail (Alexander) (1915-   ,
Birmingham, AL) professor, novelist, poet

  For My People. New Haven: Yale University Press,
   1942.

Educated in church schools of Meridian, Mississippi,
Birmingham, Alabama, and New Orleans. Attended New
Orleans   (Dillard) University, Northwestern (B.A.,
1935), and the University of Iowa (M.A., 1940; Ph.D.,
1965).   Participated in the Chicago Writers Project.
Taught   at   West Virginia State College   (1942),
Livingstone   College in Salisbury, North Carolina
(1945-1946), Jackson State University (1949-   ).
Poetry published in *Crisis* and *Poetry* magazines, and
widely anthologized.   Received a Houghton Mifflin
Literary   Fellowship   for   *Jubilee*   and the Yale
University Younger Poets Award for *For My People*
(1942).
[2, 25, 35]

Walker, Thomas Hamilton "Beb" (1873- , Tallahassee,
FL) minister

Bebbly, or the Victorious Preacher. Gainesville,
   FL: Pepper Publishing and Printing Company, 1910.
*J.Johnson, or the Unknown Man; an answer to Mr.
   Thos. Dixon's   "Sins of the Fathers"*. Deland,
   FL: E.O. Painter Printing, 1915.

Attended   public   school   in Tallahassee, Florida,
Cookman   Institute   in   Daytona   Florida,   Gammon
Theological   Seminary   (Atlanta),   College   of   West
Africa   and   College   of   Liberia.   Teacher and pastor
while   at   Cookman   Institute,   and   pastor   in
Jacksonville, Florida.   Founded   the   St. Joseph Aid
Society.   Credited   with   the   publishing   of   such
nonfiction   works   as   *The Man Without a Blemish*,
Presidents of Liberia, History of Liberia.
[57, 58]

Ward, Theodore (1908-1941, Thibodeaux, LA) playwright

Lived   on   his own at 13, working at a variety of jobs
in   a   number   of   cities   in   route   to   the   North.
Attended   the University of Utah and the University of
Wisconsin.   Worked   as   staff artist for WIDA station
in Madison, Wisconsin, instructor for the WPA, and as
an   actor.   Founded   the Negro Playwrights Company in
1940,   in   New   York.   Received the Zona Gale Creative
Writing   Scholarship   for   college   work   at   the
University   of Utah.   Contributed plays to a number of
anthologies.
[11]

Waring, Robert Lewis (1863-) novelist

   As We See It. Washington, D.C.:   Press of C.F.
   Sudworth, 1910.

Waters,   James   C.,   Jr.   (1879-   , Jacksonville, FL)
lawyer, minister

   Shame of Duluth. (n.d.)

Graduated   Haines   Institute (1897); Howard University
(A.B.,   1904;   L.L.B.,   1911).   Worked   as printer for
Georgia Baptist, Colored American (Washington, D.C.),
Afro-American   (Baltimore,   Maryland);   contributing
editor   for   the   *Washington Sun*   and   the *Washington
Eagle*;   worked   for   Civil Service in Washington, D.C.
and New Jersey; practiced law, and taught and served
as librarian at Howard University.
[57]

Watkins, Lucian Bottow (1879-1921, Chesterfield, VA)
teacher and poet

  Voices of Solitude. Chicago: M.A. Donahue and
    Co., 1903.
  Whispering Winds.
  The Old Rag Cabin (poem). Russell, Wyoming: The
    Printry, 1910.

Educated in Chesterfield and at Virginia Normal and
Industrial Institute in Petersburg. Taught school;
served in WWI.
[34]

Wheeler,   Benjamin   (1854-1919,   Charlotte,   NC)
minister, poet

  Cullings from Zion's Poets. Mobile AL: n.p., 1907.
  The Varick Family. Mobile: n.p., 1907.

Attended   schools   sponsored   by   Freedman's
Association. Worked in South Carolina for a while,
then went to New York where he was converted in the
Mother Zion Church; pastored in New Jersey, New York
and Alabama.
[21]

Wheeler, Charles Enoch (1901- , Augusta, GA) poet

  Prelude (a book of poems). Privately issued, 1943.

Attended private school in Augusta and New York.
Contributed to *Crisis*.

White,   Walter (1893-1955, Atlanta, GA) novelist,
civil rights activist

  Fire in the Flint. 1924. rpt. New York: Negro
    Universities Press, 1969.
  Flight. 1926. rpt. New York: Negro Universities
    Press, 1964.

Graduated from Atlanta University (B.A., 1916); post
graduate work in economics and sociology in the
College of the City of New York.   Worked as
assistant secretary for NAACP (1918-1931) and as
secretary of the NAACP (1931-1955). Received honorary
LL.D. from Howard University (1939), Guggenheim
Foundation Fellowship (1927, 1928), Spingharn Medal
(1937). Nonfiction: *Rope and Faggot: A Biography of*

Judge Lynch (1929, 1969), *A Rising Wind* (1948, 1969), and *How Far the Promised Land?* (1955). Published articles in *Survey, The Nation, American Mercury, Century, Harper's Magazine, Congressional Digest, Saturday Evening Post, Survey Graphic.*
[42, 36]

Whitfield, Cupid Aleyus (1868- , Gadsden County, FL) clergyman, poet

   Poems of Today, or Some from the Everglades.

Attended school in Gadsden county; graduated from the State Agricultural and Mechanical College (Tallahassee, Florida) and Morris Brown College (D.D., 1906). Taught in Gadsden County. Ordained A.M.E. deacon in 1899 and A.M.E. Bishop in 1901 in Marianna. Pastored in Florida and Mississippi. Professor of English Literature and Ancient History (1910-1911) at and principal of Edward Waters College in Jacksonville, Florida (1911-1912). Served as Florida Conference missionary.
[58]

Whitman, Albery A. (1851-1901, Montfordsville, Hart County, KY) evangelist, educator, poet

   Leelah Misled. Elizabethtown, KY: Richard LaRue, 1873.
   Not a Man and Yet a Man. Springfield, Ohio: Republic Printing, 1877.
   The Rape of Florida. St. Louis: Nixon-Jones Printing, 1884.
   Twasinta's Seminoles; or Rape of Florida. St. Louis: Nixon and Jones Printing Co., 1885.
   The World's Fair Poems: The Freedmen's Triumphant Song. Atlanta: Halsey, July 1893.
   An Idyll of the South. New York: Metaphysical Publishing Co., 1901.

Studied under Bishop Daniel A. Payne at Wilberforce University, Ohio. Worked first in shops and on railroads in Kentucky and Ohio, before becoming A.M.E. minister in Springfield, Ohio, Kansas, and Savannah, Georgia.
[36, 42, 46, 49]

Williams, Lucy Ariel (See Holloway, Lucy Ariel Williams.)

Wilson,   Harriet   (1808-1870,   Fredericksburg,   VA)
novelist

  *Our Nig: Or Sketches from the Life of a Free Black
  in a Two-Story White House, Showing that Slavery's
  Shadow Falls Over There, by "Our Nig".* Boston:
  George C. Rand and Avery, 1859.
  Our Nig, ed. Henry Gates, Jr. New York: Random
  House, 1983.

[Introduction to 1983 edition of *Our Nig*]

Wood,   Charles   Winter   (1870- , Nashville, TN) actor,
professor, playwright-director

  College Life (n.d.)
  In Defense of Him. (n.d.)

Attended Beloit College in Beloit, Wisconsin (B.A.,
1895;   M.A.,   1898),   Chicago   Theological   Seminary
(D.D., 1898), and Columbia University.   Taught at
Tuskegee Institute (1898-1901) and at Florida A&M;
Northern Financial Secretary (1904-1926). Director
of the Tuskegee Players.
[57]

Wood,   John   Wesley   (1865- , Tolbert   County,   GA)
bishop, public school teacher, poet

  Lyrics of Sunshine.   Hord Brothers, 1922.

Educated at LaGrange Academy (1882), Morris Brown
College (1896), Moody Bible School, Chicago (1911-
1912); Livingstone College (D.D., 1912). Taught in
the public schools of Marietta, Georgia; A.M.E.
bishop in Georgia.
[57]

Wright, Richard (1908-1960, Roxie, MS) novelist

  Bright and Morning Star. New York: International
  Publishers, 1938.
  Uncle Tom's Children. New York: Harper and Bros.,
  1938.
  Native Son. New York: Harper, 1940.
  The Outsider. New York: Harper, 1953.

No formal education. Participated in Chicago Federal
Writers Project and helped to write with other
writers in the New York Writers Project a *Guide to*

Harlem (1930s). Received the *Story Magazine* prize for "Fire and Cloud" (1938) Guggenheim Fellowship (1939); and the Spingarn Medal (1940). Nonfiction works include *Black Boy* (1943), *Twelve Million Black Voices* (1941), *Black Power* (1954), *White Man, Listen* (1957), *The Color Curtain* (1956), *Pagan Spain* (1957). Contributed to *Daily Worker*, and *Black Masses*. Fiction after 1953: *Savage Holiday* (1954), *The Long Dream* (1958), *Eight Men* (1961), *Lawd Today* (1963).
[2, 36, 42, 49]

Wright, Julius C. (1886- , AL) poet

  Poetic Diamonds. Montgomery, AL: W.E. Allred
    Printing, 1906.
[Introduction to *Poetic Diamonds*]

Wright, Sarah Elizabeth (1929- , Eastern Shore, MD) critic poet, novelist

  (In anthologies published before 1953)

Studied at Howard University, the University of Pennsylvania, and Cheney State Teachers College. Wrote *This Child's Gonna Live* (1969).
[44]

Yancey, Bessie Woodson (1882- , New Canton, Buckingham County, VA) educator, poet

  Echoes from the Hills, A Book of Poems.
    Washington, D.C.: The Associated Publishing, 1939.

Attended rural school in New Canton; diploma from Douglas High School in Huntington, West Virginia where her brother Carter G. Woodson was principal (1901). Teacher in mining camp near Montgomery, West Virginia and Guyandore, West Virginia.
[Introduction to *Echoes*]

Yerby, Frank (1916- , Augusta, GA) teacher, novelist

  Foxes of Harrow. New York: Dial, 1946.
  The Vixens. New York: Dial, 1947.
  The Golden Hawk. New York: Dial, 1948.
  Pride's Castle. New York: Dial, 1949.
  Floodtide. New York: Dial, 1950.
  The Saracen Blade. New York: Dial, 1952.
  The Devil's Laughter. New York: Dial, 1953.

Attended Paine College (B.A., 1937), Fisk University (M.A., 1938), and the University of Chicago. Taught at Florida A&M College (1939-1940) and Southern University in Baton Rouge, Louisiana (1940-1941); worked during the war at Ford Motor Company in Dearborn, Michigan (1942-1944) and Ranger aircraft in Jamaica, New York (1944-1945). Fulltime writer after 1945, publishing numerous novels including *Benton's Row* (1954), *Bride of Liberty* (1954), *A Woman Called Fancy* (1954), *The Treasure of Pleasant Valley* (1955), *Captain Rebel* (1956), *Fairoaks* (1957), *The Serpent and the Staff* (1958), *Jarrett's Jade* (1959), *Gillian* (1960), *The Garfield Honor* (1961), *Griffin's Way* (1962), *Old Gods Laugh* (1964), *An Odor of Sanctity* (1965), *Goat Song* (1968), *Judas, My Brother* (1968), *Speak Now* (1969), *The Dahomean* (1971), *The Girl from Storyville* (1972), *The Voyage Unplanned* (1972), *Tobias and the Angel* (1975), *A Rose for Ana Maria* (1976).
[2, 42, 49]

Appendixes

Author Listing By State

Alabama
Alba, Nanina
Alexander, Truman Hudson
Allen, Junius Mordecai
Andrews, W.T.
Benjamin, R.C.O.
Brown, Handy Nereus
Carmicheal, Waverly Turner
Clarke, John Henrik
Cuthbert, Marion
Delaney, Clarissa M. Scott
Finch, Amanda
Finch, Giles
Handy, William C.
Harris, Leon R.
Henderson, George W.
Hollaway, Lucy Ariel Williams
McCall, James Edward
Mitchell, Loften
Newsome, Effie L.
Shackleford, William H.
Tarry, Ellen
Thomas, Joseph Turner
Walker, Margaret
Wright, Julius C.

Delaware
Redding, J. Saunders

Florida
Butler, Alpheus
Cheriot, Henri
Fields, Maurice
Fortune, Timothy Thomas
Gilbert, Mercedes
Hurston, Zora Neale
Johnson, James Weldon
Menard, John Willis
Morse, Leonard Francis
Reason, Arthur W.
Silvera, Edward S.
Walker, Thomas Hamilton
Waters, James C., Jr.

Whitfield, Cupid Aleyus

Georgia
Albert, Octavia V. Rogers
Arneaux, J.A.
Borders, William Holmes
Braithwaite, William S.B.
Cooper, Annie Julia
Curthwright, Wesley
Davis, Ossie
Dodson, Owen
Dubois, W.E.B.
Echols, Carl
Flanagan, Thomas Jefferson
Fleming, Sarah Lee Brown
Floyd, Silas X.
Heard, William
Hill, Abram
Holloway, John Wesley
Huff, William H.
Huntley, Elizabeth M.
Johnson, Georgia Douglas
Killens, John Oliver
Major, Clarence
Rowe, George C.
Tracy, Robert A.
Troup, Cornelius
Wheeler, Charles E.
White, Walter
Wood, John Wesley
Yerby, Frank

Kentucky
Boyd, Francis A.
Brown, William Wells
Cotter, Joseph S., Jr.
Cotter, Joseph S., Sr.
Danner, Margaret
Gunner, Mary Frances
Laine, Henry Allen
Means, Sterling
Poston, Theodore
Stowers, Walter H.
Whitman, Albery A.

Louisiana
Bibb, Eloise Thompson
Bontemps, Arna
Burroughs, Margaret G.
Christian, Marcus Bruce

Clark, Peter Wellington
Collins, Leslie Morgan
Felton, Haleemon Shaik
Graham, Lorenz Bell
Imbert, Dennis I.
Jonas, Rosalie
Lanusse, Armand
Menard, John Willis
McCarthy, Eugene V.
Nelson, Alice Ruth Moore Dunbar
Rillieux, Victor-Ernest
Sejour, Victor
Shine, Ted
Thierry, Camille
Tyler, Ephrain D.
Ward, Theodore

Maryland
Bruce, John Edward
Fernandis, Sarah Collins
Fowler, Charles
Harper, Frances W.
Hill, William Allyn
Turpin, Waters E.
Wright, Sarah E.

Mississippi
Attaway, William A.
Battle, Effie Dean
Beadle, Samuel A.
Brooks, Jonathan Henderson
Butler, Samuel S.
Coffin, Frank Barbour
Hall, Josie B.
Hill, Julious
Holman, M. Carl
Jenkins, Deadrick F.
Jones, Edward S.
Kinds, Levander
Lee, George Washington
Pawley, Thomas D., Jr.
Pitts, Richard
Wright, Richard

North Carolina
Allen, George Leonard
Bond, Frederick W.
Brown, Charlotte Hawkins
Chestnutt, Charles W.
Corbett, Maurice

Davis, Daniel W.
Forster, Estelle Ancrum
Gordon, Charles B.
Hawkins, Walter E.
Hayes, Donald J.
Heard, Josie D.H.
Horton, George Moses
Johnson, Edward A.
Johnson, Maggie Pogue
Lipscomb, Edward Hart
Love, Ruth Leary
Martin, John Sella
McGirt, James E.
Richardson, Willis
Smith, Lucy Smith
Smith, S.P.
Walden, Islay
Wheeler, Benjamin

South Carolina
Ayers, Virginia
Barber, J. Max
Brawley, Benjamin
Brownlee, Julius P.
Dinkins, Charles R.
Ford, Nick Aaron
Fordham, Mary W.
Jones, Joshua Henry, Jr.
Mayfield, Julian
McBrown, Gertrude Simmons
Payne, Daniel A.
Pickens, William
Turner, Henry McNeal

Tennessee
Banks, William A.
Brooks, Rosa Paul
Christian, Ethel L. Perry
Clem, Charles D.
Coleman, Jamye H.
Fabio, Sarah Webster
Fisher, Leland M.
Franklin, James Thomas
Gloster, Hugh
Griggs, Sutton
Hayden, Robert
Jamison, Roscoe Conkling
Lane, James Franklin
Lyles, Aubrey
Majors, Monroe Alpheus

McClellan, George M.
Miller, Clifford
Miller, Flournoy
Rogers, Alex
Tolson, Melvin
Wood, Charles Winter

Virginia
Ashby, William
Benjamin, R.C.O.
Brooks, Walter Henderson
Cannon, David W., Jr.
Dett, Nathaniel
Dismond, H. Binga
Edmonds, Randolph
Hill, John H.
Hill, Leslie P.
Johnson, Charles S.
Johnson, Helen Aurelia
Johnson, Herbert C.
Lee, John Francis
Long, Naomi (Madgett)
Nash, Theodore E.D.
Powell, Adam Clayton, Sr.
Ragland, J. Farley
Ridout, Daniel Lyman
Rowe, George C.
Spencer, Anne
Thomas, David Gatewood
Tinsley, Tomi
Watkins, Lucian Bottow
Wilson, Harriet
Yancy, Bessie Woodson

Washington, D.C.
Alexander, Lewis
Bohanan, Otto Leland
Bonner, Marita
Brown, Sterling
Bruce, Richard
Butcher, James W., Jr.
Carter, Herman J.D.
Clifford, Carrie W.
Cook, Mercer
Cuney, Waring
Dodson, Owen
Dreer, Herman
Fisher, Rudolph
Grimke, Angelina Weld
Miller, May

Morrison, William Lorenzo
Murphy, Beatrice
Razafenkariefo, Andrea
Todd, Walter
Toomer, Jean
Vashon, George B.

West Virginia
Campbell, James Edwin
Delaney, Martin R.
Demby, William
Dickerson, Noy Jasper
Jones, J. McHenry
Matheus, John F.

Author Listing By Period

1829-1865
Allen, J. Mordecai
Brown, William Wells
Delaney, Martin R.
Harper, Frances W.
Payne, Daniel A.
Sejour, Victor
Wilson, Harriet
Lanusse, Armand
Martin, John Sella
McCarthy, Eugene V.

1866-1912
Albert, Octavia V. Rogers
Beadel, Samuel A.
Benjamin, R.C.O.
Bibb, Eloise Thompson
Boyd, Francis A.
Braithwaite, William S.B.
Brawley, Benjamin
Brown, Handy Nereus
Brown, William Wells
Butler, Samuel B.
Campbell, James Edwin
Chestnutt, Charles W.
Clem, Charles D.
Clifford, Carrie W.
Cooper, Anna Julia
Cotter, Jospeh S., Sr.
Davis, Daniel W.
Dett, R. Nathaniel

Dinkins, Charles R.
DuBois, W.E.B.
Fisher, Leland M.
Floyd, Silas X.
Fordham, Mary Weston
Fortune, Timothy Thomas
Fowler, Charles Henry
Franklin, James Thomas
Gilmore, F. Grant
Griggs, Sutton
Heard, Josie D.
Harper, Francis W. Harper
Horton, George M.
Johnson, Edward Augustus
Johnson, James Weldon
Johnson, Maggie Pogue
Jones, Edward Smythe
Jones, J. McHenry
Lee, John Francis
McGirt, James E.
Nash, T.E.D.
Nelson, Alice R.M.D.
Payne, Daniel A.
Rogers, Alex
Rowe, George C.
Shackleford, Otis M.
Shackleford, William H.
Stowers, Walter
Thomas, Joseph Turner
Todd, Walter E.
Turner, Henry McNeal
Vashon, George B.
Walker, Thomas H.
Waring, Robert L.
Watkins, Lucian Bottow
Wheeler, Benjamin
Whitman, Albery A.
Wright, Julius C.

1913-1928
Albert, Octavia V. Rogers
Alexander, Lewis
Ashby, William M.
Battle, Effie D.
Bibb, Eloise Thompson
Bohanan, Otto
Braithwaite, William S.
Brawley, Benjamin
Brown, Charlotte Hawkins
Brownlee, Julius P.

Bruce, John Edward
Bruce, Richard
Carmicheal, Waverly Turner
Cheriot, Henri
Clifford, Carrie Williams
Corbett, Maurice
Cotter, Joseph S., Jr.
Cotter, Joseph S., Sr.
Delaney, Clarissa S.
Dickerson, Noy Jasper
Dreer, Herman
DuBois, W.E.B.
Fernandis, Sarah C.
Fisher, Rudolph
Flanagan, Thomas
Gordon, Charles B.
Graham, Lorenz Bell
Grimke, Angelina Weld
Gunner, Mary Frances
Hall, Josie B.
Hawkins, Walter Everette
Hill, Julious
Hill, Leslie P.
Holloway, John W.
Jamison, Roscoe C.
Johnson, Charles S.
Johnson, Georgia D.
Johnson, James Weldon
Johnson, Maggie Pogue
Jonas, Rosalie
Jones, Joshua Henry, Jr.
Laine, Henry Allen
Lipscomb, Edward H.
Majors, Monroe Alpheus
Matheus, John Frederick
McCall, James E.
McClellan, George M.
Means, Sterling
Miller, Clifford
Miller, Flournoy
Morse, Loenard
Morton, Lena B.
Newsome, Effie L.
Pickens, William
Ridout, Daniel L.
Rogers, Alex
Shackleford, Otis
Shackleford, William
Smith, S.P.
Todd, Walter E.

Toomer, Jean
Tracy, Robert
Tyler, Ephrain D.
Walker, Thomas H.
Whitfield, Cupid A.
Wood, Charles Winter
Wood, John Wesley

1929-1953
Alba, Nanina
Alexander, Truman Hudson
Attaway, William A.
Ayers, Vivian
Banks, William A.
Bohanan, Otto
Bond, Frederick W.
Bonner, Marita
Bontemps, Arna
Borders, William Holmes
Braithwaite, William S.
Brooks, Jonathan H.
Brooks, Rosa Paul
Brooks, Walter H.
Brown, Sterling
Burroughs, Margaret G.
Butcher, James W., Jr.
Butler, Alpheus
Cannon, David W., Jr.
Carter, Herman J.D.
Christian, Marcus
Clarke, John Henrik
Clark, Peter Wellington
Coleman, Jamye
Collins, Leslie Morgan
Cook, Mercer
Cuney, Waring
Cuthbert, Marion V.
Curtwright, Wesley
Danner, Margaret
Davis, Ossie
Demby, Wiliam
Dickerson, Noy Jasper
Dismond, H. Binga
Dodson, Owen
Edmonds, Randolph
Fabio, Sarah W.
Felton, Haleemon S.
Fields, Maurice
Finch, Amanda
Fisher, Rudolph

Flanagan, Thomas
Fleming, Sarah L.B.
Floyd, Silas X.
Ford, Nick Aaron
Forster, Estelle Ancrum
Gholson, E.
Gilbert, Mercedes
Gilmore, F. Grant
Gloster, Hugh
Handy, William C.
Harris, Leon R.
Hayden, Robert
Hayes, Donald Jeffrey
Heard, William
Henderson, George Wylie
Hill, John H.
Hill, William Allyn
Hollaway, Lucy A.W.
Holman, M. Carl
Huff, William
Huntley, Elizabeth M.
Hurston, Zora Neale
Jenkins, Deadrick
Johnson, Helen Aurelia
Johnson, Herbert Clark
Johnson, James Weldon
Kinds, Levander
Killens, John O.
Lane, James Franklin
Lee, George Washington
Love, Ruth Leary
Lyles, Aubrey
Madgett, Naomi Long
Mayfield, Julian
McBrown, Gertrude
Miller, Clifford
Miller, Flournoy
Miller, May
Miller, Kelly
Mitchell, Loften
Morrison, William Lorenzo
Morton, Lena B.
Murphy, Beatrice
Pitts, Richard
Poston, Theodore
Powell, Adam Clayton, Sr.
Ragland, J. Farley
Razafenkeriefo, Andrea
Reason, Arthur
Redding, J. Saunders

Richardson, Willis
Shaw, O'Wendell
Shine, Ted
Silvera, Edward
Smith, Lucy
Spencer, Anne
Thomas, David G.
Tinsley, Tomi C.
Tolson, Melvin
Troup, C.V.
Turpin, Waters E.
Walker, Margaret
Ward, Theodore
Wheeler, Charles Enoch
White, Walter
Wright, Richard
Wright, Sarah E.
Yancey, Bessie W.
Yerby, Frank

Selected Bibliography of
Southern Black Writers,
1829–1953

Albert, Octavia V. Rogers. *The House of Bondage, or Charlotte Brooks and Other Slaves*. New York: Hunt and Eaton, 1890.

Alexander, Truman Hudson. *Loot*. 1932. rpt. Freeport, NY: Books for Libraries Press, 1972.

Allen, Junius Mordecai. *Rhymes, Tales and Rhymed Tales*. Topeka, KS: Crane & Co., 1906.

Andrews, W.T. *A Waif--a Prince; or A Mother's Triumph*. Freeport, NY: Books for Libraries Press, 1972.

Ashby, William M. *Redder Blood*. New York: Cosmopolitan, 1915.
The Road to Damascus. Boston: Christopher, 1935.

Attaway, William Alexander. *Let Me Breathe Thunder*. New York: Doubleday and Doran, 1939.
Blood on the Forge. New York: Doubleday, 1941.

Ayers, Vivian. *Spice Dawns*. New York: Exposition, 1953.
Bow Boly (play), n.p.

Banks, William Augustus. *Gathering Dusk*. Chattanooga, TN: The Wilson Printing Co., 1935.
Lest We Forget. Chattanooga, TN: Central High Press, 1930.
Beyond the Rockies and Other Poems. Philadelphia: Doran & Co., 1926.

Battle, Effie Dean Threat. *Gleanings from Dixieland*. Tuskegee Institute, AL: Tuskegee Institute, 1914.

Beadle, Samuel A. *Sketches from Life in Dixie*. Chicago: Scroll Publishing and Literary Syndicate, 1899.
Adam Shuffler. Jackson, MS: Harmon Publishing Co., 1901.
Lyrics from the Underworld. Jackson, MS: W.A. Scott, 1912.

Benjamin, Robert C.O. *Poetic Gems*. Charlotteville, VA: Peck and Allen Printers, 1883.

The Defender of Obadiah Cuff. (n.d.)

Bibb, Eloise Thompson. *Poems*. 1895. rpt. Freeport, NY: Books for Libraries Press, 1971.

Bond, Frederick W. *Family Affair*; a one act play. [Institute]: West Virginia State College, 1939.

Bontemps, Arna Wendell. *God Sends Sunday*. New York: Harcourt, Brace and Co., 1931.
You Can't Pet a Possum. New York: W. Morrow and Co., 1934.
Black Thunder. 1936. rpt. Boston: Beacon Press, 1968.
Sad-faced Boy. Boston: Houghton Mifflin, 1937.
Drums at Dusk. New York: Macmillan, 1939.
_____and Langston Hughes. *Popo and Fifina, Children of Haiti*. New York: Macmillan Co., 1932.
_____. *St. Louis Woman*. 1946.
_____and Jack Conroy. *The Fast Sooner Hound*. 1942.
_____. *Slappy Hooper, the Wonderful Sign Painter*. Boston: Houghton Mifflin, 1946.

Borders, William Holmes. *Thunderbolts*. Atlanta: Morris Brown College Press, 1942.

Boyd, Francis A. *Columbiana; or the North Star*. Chicago: Steam and Job Printing House of B. Hand, 1870.

Braithwaite, William Stanley Beaumont. *The Canadian*. Boston: Small, Maynard, and Co., 1901.
Lyrics of Life and Love. Boston: H.B. Turner and Co., 1904.
The House of Falling Leaves with Other Poems. Boston: J.W. Luce and Co., 1908.
Going Over Tindel. Boston: B.J. Brimmer Co., 1924.
Selected Poems. New York: Coward-McCann, Inc., 1948.

Brawley, Benjamin. *A Prayer*. Atlanta: Atlanta Baptist College Press, 1899.
A Toast to Love and Death. Atlanta: Atlanta Baptist College Press, 1902.
The Problem and Other Poems. Washington, D.C.: Author, 1911.
The Seven Sleepers of Ephesus. Atlanta: Foster and Davies, 1917.

Brooks, Jonathan Henderson. *The Resurrection and*

Other Poems. Dallas: Kaleidoscope Press, 1948.

Brooks, Rosa Paul. *Poetic Meditations*. 1945.

Brooks, Walter Henderson. *Original Poems*.
   Washington, D.C.: The Sunday School of the Church
   in connection with his 50th anniversary as pastor,
   1932.
   The   Pastor's   Voice,   a   Collection   of   Poems.
   Washington, D.C.: Associated, 1945.

Brown, Charlotte Hawkins. *"Mammy," a Story of Negro
   Fidelity and Southern Neglect*. Pilgrim Press,
   1919.

Brown, Handy Nereus. *The Necromancer*. 1904. rpt.
   New York: AMS Press, 1970.

Brown, Sterling. *Southern Road*. New York:
   Harcourt, Brace and Co., 1932.

Brown, William Wells. *The Anti-Slavery Harp: A
   Collection of Songs for Anti-Slavery Meetings*.
   Boston: B.J. Marsh, 1848.
   *Clotel; or the President's Daughter: A Narrative
   of Slave Life in the United States*. 1853. rpt.
   New York: Arno Press, 1969.
   *Experience; Or, How to Give a Northern Man a
   Backbone*. 1856.
   *The Escape; or a Leap for Freedom, a drama in five
   acts*. Boston: R.F. Walcut, 1858.
   *Miralda; or, the Beautiful Quadroon. A Romance of
   Slavery.   Founded in Fact*. Published weekly in the
   Anglo- African, November 30-March 16, 1860-1861.
   Clotelle: A   Tale of the Southern States. 1864.
   rpt. Boston: James Redpath, 1955.
   *Clotelle; or, the Colored Heroine.   A Tale of
   Southern States*. 1867. rpt. Miami: Mnemosyne
   Publishing, Inc., 1969.

Brownlee, Julius Pinkney. *Ripples*. Anderson, SC:
   Cox Stationery Co., 1914.

Bruce, John Edward. *The Awakening of Hezekiah Jones*.
   Hopkinsville, KY: Phil H. Brown, 1916.
   Selected Writings (ed. by Peter Gilbert). New
   York: Arno Press, 1971.

Burroughs, Margaret G. *Jasper the Drummin' Boy*. New
   York: Viking, 1947.

Butcher, James W., Jr. *The Seer*. In *Negro Caravan*,
    1941.
    Milk and Honey (play), n.d.

Butler, Alpheus. *Make Way for Happiness*. Boston:
    Christopher, 1932.
    Sepia Vistas. New York: Exposition Press, 1941.

Butler, Samuel S. *Wit and Humor*. Edwards, MS: New
    Light Steam Press, 1911.

Campbell, James Edwin. *Driftings and Gleanings*.
    Chicago: The Author, 1888.
    Echoes from the Cabin and Elsewhere. Chicago:
    The Author, 1895.

Cannon, David Wadsworth, Jr. *Black Labor Chant and
    Other Poems*. New York: The National Council on
    Religion in Higher Education, 1939.

Carmicheal, Waverly Turner. *From the Heart of a
    Folk. A Book of Songs*. Boston: Cornhill, 1918.

Carter, Herman J.D. *The Scottsboro Blues*. Nashville:
    The Mahlon Publishing Co., 1933.

Cheriot, Henri. *Black Ink*. Orlando, FL: Henri
    Cheriot Publishing Co., 1917.

Chestnutt, Charles W. *The Wife of His Youth and Other
    Stories of the Color Line*. Boston: Houghton
    Mifflin, 1899.
    The Conjure Woman. New York: Houghton Mifflin,
    1899.
    The House Behind the Cedars. Boston: Houghton
    Mifflin, 1900.
    The Marrow of Tradition. Boston: Houghton
    Mifflin, 1901.
    The Colonel's Dream. New York: Doubleday, Page,
    and Co., 1905.
Christian, Ethel L. Perry. *American Sunbursts*. n.p.

Clarke, John Henrik. *Rebellion in Rhyme*. Prairie
    City, IL: Decker Press, 1948.

Clem, Charles Douglas. *Rhymes of a Rhymster*. Edmond,
    OK: Author, 1901.
    A Little Souvenir. n.p., 1908.
    Booker T. Washington, A Poem. n.d.

Clifford, Carrie Williams. *Race Rhymes*. Washington,
    D.C.: Pendleton, 1911.

The Widening Light. Boston: Walter   Reid   Co.,
1922.

Coffin, Frank Barbour. *Coffin's Poems with Ajax's
Ordeal*. Little Rock, Ark.:   Colored Advocate,
1897.
Factum   Factorum. New York: New Haven Press,
1947.

Coleman, Jamye H. *Songs of My Soul*. n.p.
Cries from the Cross (meditations). n.p.

Collins, Leslie Morgan. *Exile, a Book of Verse*.
Atlanta: The B.F. Logan Press, 1938.

Cooper, Anna Julia. *A Voice from the South*. Xenia,
OH: 1892.
Christmas Plays. (no imprint)

Corbett, Maurice. *The Harp of Ethiopia*. Nashville:
National Baptist Publishing Board, 1914.

Cotter, Joseph, Jr. *The Band of Gideon and Other
Lyrics*. Boston: Cornhill, 1918.

Cotter, Joseph, Sr. *A Rhyming*. Louisville, KY: New
South Publishing, 1895.
Links of Friendship. Louisville, KY: The Bradley
and Gilbert Co., 1898.
A White Song and a Black One. Louisville, KY:
The Bradley and Gilbert Co., 1909.
Negro Tales. 1912. rpt. Miami: Mnemosyne
Publishing Co., 1969.
Collected Poems of Joseph S. Cotter. New York:
Henry Harrison, 1938.
*Sequel to the "Pied Piper of Hamelin" and Other
Poems*. New York: Harrison, 1939.
Caleb, the Degenerate. New York: Harrison, 1940.

Cuthbert, Marion Vera. *Songs of Creation*. New York:
Women's Press, 1949.

Davis, Daniel W. *Idle Moments; Containing
Emancipation and Other Poems*. Baltimore, MD: The
Educators of Morgan College, 1895.
'Weh Down Souf, and Other Poems. Cleveland, OH:
Helman-Taylor Co., 1897.

Davis, Ossie. *Goldbrickers*. 1944.
Alice in Wonder. 1953.

Delaney, Martin Robinson. *Blake, or the Huts of America*. 1859. rpt. NY: Arno Press, 1969.

Demby, William. *Beetlecreek*. New York: Rhinehart, 1950.

Dett, Robert Nathaniel. *Album of the Heart*. 1911.

Dickerson, Noy Jasper. *Original Poetry*. Bluefield, WVA: Author, 1927.
A Scrapbook. Boston: The Christopher Publishing House, 1931.

Dinkins, Charles R. *Lyrics of Love*. Columbia, SC: The State Co., 1904.

Dismond, H. Binga. *We Who Would Die and Other Poems*. New York: Malliett and Co., 1943.

Dodson, Owen. *Including Laughter*. 1936.
Gargoyles in Florida. 1936.
Divine Comedy. 1938.
The Garden of Time. 1939.
Amistad. 1939.
The Southern Star. 1940.
Doomsday. 1941.
Everybody Join Hands. 1942.
Someday We're Gonna Tear the Pillars Down. 1942.
Freedom the Banner. 1942.
The Ballad of Dorrie Miller. 1942.
New World A-Coming. 1944.
Powerful Long Ladder. New York: Farar, Strauss, 1946.
Bayou Legend. 1946.
The Third Fourth of July. 1946.

Dreer, Herman. *The Immediate Jewel of His Soul*. St. Louis: The St. Louis Argus Publishing Co., 1919.

DuBois, William E.B. *The Quest of the Silver Fleece*. 1911. rpt. College Park, MD: McGrath Publishing Co., 1969.
Dark Princess. 1928. rpt. New York: Harcourt, Brace and Co., 1970.

Edmonds, Randolph. *Shades and Shadows*. Boston: Meador Publishing Co., 1930.
Six Plays for the Negro Theatre. Boston: Walter Baker Co., 1934.
The Land of Cotton and Other Plays. Washington, D.C.: Associated Publishers, 1952.

Earth and Stars: A Problem Play Concerning Negro and White Leadership in the South. Tallahassee: n.p., 1961.

Fields, Maurice. *The Collected Poems of Maurice C. Fields*. New York: The Exposition Press, 1940.
Testament of Youth. New York: Pegasus Publishing Co., 1941.

Finch, Amanda. *Black Trail: A Novella of Love in the South*. New York: William-Frederick Press, 1951.

Finch, Giles. *A Collection of 75 Original Poems*. Birmingham, AL: Author, 1955.

Fisher, Rudolph. *The Walls of Jericho*. New York: Knopf, 1928.
The Conjure Man Dies, a Mystery Tale of Dark Harlem. New York: Covici-Friede, 1932.

Flanagan, Thomas Jefferson. *By the Pine Knot Torches*. Atlanta: The Dickcut Co., 1921.
The Harvest Hymn. Atlanta: Privately Printed, n.d.
The Road to Mount McKeithan. Atlanta: Independent Publishers Corporation, 1927.
Smilin' Thru the Corn and Other Verse. Atlanta: Independent Publishers, 1927.
The Canyons of Providence. Atlanta: The Author, 1941.

Fleming, Sarah Lee Brown. *Clouds of Sunshine*. Boston: Cornhill, 1920.
Hope's Highway. New York: The Neale Publishing Co., 1918.

Floyd, Silas X. *Floyd's Flowers*. 1905. rpt. New York: AMS Press, 1970.
Short Stories for Colored People, Both Old and Young. n.p.: 1920.

Ford, Nick Aaron. *Songs from the Dark: Original Poems*. Boston: Meador, 1940.

Fordham, Mary Weston. *Magnolia Leaves*. Charleston, SC: Walker, Evans and Cogswell Co., 1897.

Forster, Estelle Ancrum. *A Dream of Enchantment*. Boston: Theo. Presser, 1926.

Fortune, Timothy Thomas. *Dreams of Life:*

Miscellaneous Poems. New York: Fortune and Peterson, 1905.

Fowler, Charles Henry. *Historical Romance of the American Negro*. Baltimore, MD: Press of Thomas and Evans, 1902.

Franklin, James Thomas. *Jessamine Poems*. Memphis, TN: Tracy Printing, 1900.
Mid-Day Gleanings, a Book for Home and Holiday Reading. Memphis, TN: Tracy Printing, 1893.

Gholson, E. *Musings of a Minister*. Boston: Christopher, 1943.
From Jerusalem to Jericho. Boston: Chapman and Grimes, 1943.

Gilbert, Mercedes. *Selected Gems of Poetry, Comedy and Drama*. Boston: Christopher, 1931.
Aunt Sara's Wooden God. Boston: Christopher, 1938.

Gilmore, F. Grant. *Masonic and Other Poems*. The Author, n.p., 1908.
The Problem; a Military Novel. 1915. rpt. College Park, MD: McGrath Publishing Co., 1969.

Graham, Lorenz Bell. *How God Fix Jonah*. New York: Reynal, 1946.
Every Man Heart Lay Down. New York: Crowell, 1946.
God Wash the World and Start Again. New York: Crowell, 1946.
Tales of Momolu. New York: Reynal, 1946.

Griggs, Sutton. *Imperium in Imperio*. 1899. rpt. Miami: Mnemosyne, 1969.
Overshadowed. 1901. rpt. New York: AMS Press, 1970.
Unfettered. 1902. rpt. New York: AMS Press, 1970.
The Hindered Hand; or the Reign of the Repressionist. 1905. rpt. Miami: Mnemosyne, 1969.
Pointing the Way. 1908. rpt. New York: AMS Press, 1970.
Wisdom's Call. 1911. rpt. Miami: Mnemosyne, 1969.

Grimke, Angelina Weld. *Rachel: A Play in Three Acts*. 1920. rpt. College Park, MD: McGrath Publishing Co., 1969.

Gunner, Mary Frances. *The Light of a Woman*. n.p.

Handy, William Christopher. *Truth in Rhyme, and Miscellaneous Prose Compositions*. U.S.: Caxton Press, 1928.

Harper, Frances E. Watkins. *Poems on Miscellaneous Subjects*. Boston: J.B. Yerrington and Sons, Printers, 1854.
Moses: A Story of the Nile. Philadelphia: Merrihew and Sons Printers, 1869.
Poems. Philadelphia: Merrihew and Sons Printers, 1871.
Sketches of Southern Life. Philadelphia: Merrihew and Sons Printers, 1872.
The Martyr of Alabama and Other Poems. 1872. (no imprint)
Iola Leroy or Shadows Uplifted. 1892. College Park, MD: McGrath, 1969.
The Sparrows Fall and Other Poems. n.d.
Poems. (n.p.) 1898.
Atlanta Offering Poems. Philadelphia: The Author, 1895.
Light Beyond Darkness. n.d.
Idylls of the Bible. Philadelphia: the Author, 1901.

Harris, Leon R. *The Steelmakers and Other War Poems*. Portsmouth, OH: T.C. McConnell Printry, 1918.
Locomotive Puffs from the Back Shop. Boston: B. Humphries, 1946.
I Am a Railroad Man. Los Angeles, CA: the Author, 1948.

Hawkins, Walter Everette. *Song of the Night Child*. Wilmington, NC: n.p., 1916.
Chords and Discords. Boston: R.G. Badger, 1920.
The Child of the Night. (n.d.)
The Black Soldiers. (n.d.)
Where the Air of Freedom Is. (n.d.)
Guardian. (n.d.)
Love's Unchangeableness. (n.d.)
Too Much Religion. (n.d.)

Hayden, Robert. *Heart-Shape in the Dust*. Detroit: *The Falcon Press*, 1940.
The Lion and the Archer. Nashville: Hemphill Press, 1948.

Heard, Josie Delphine. *Morning Glories*. Lancaster,

PA: Speaker Printer, 1890.

Heard, William. *From Slavery to Bishophric in the AME Church*. 1924. rpt. New York: Arno Press, 1969.

Henderson, George Wylie. *Ollie Miss*. New York: Frederick A. Stokes Co., 1935.
Jule. New York: Creative Age Press, Inc., 1946.

Hill, Abram. *Liberty Deferred* (n.d.)
Stealing Lightning, 1937.
Hell's Half Acre, 1938.
So Shall You Reap, 1938.
Striver's Row: A Comedy About Sophisticated Harlem, 1940.
Walk Hard, 1944.
Miss Mabel, 1951.

Hill, John H. *Princess Malah*. Washington: Associated Publishers, 1933.

Hill, Julious. *The Up Reach*. Meridian MS: Tell Farmer Printer and Binder, 1923.
A Sooner Song. New York: Empire Publishing Co., 1935.
A Song of Magnolia. Boston: Meador Publishing Co., 1937.

Hill, Leslie P. *The Wings of Oppression*. Boston: Stratford, 1921.
Toussaint L'Ouverture--a Dramatic History. Boston: Christopher, 1928.

Holloway, Lucy Ariel. *Shape Them into Dreams: Poems*. New York: Exposition Press, 1955.

Holloway, John Wesley. *From the Desert*. New York: Neal Co., 1919.
Bandanas. Durham: Barber College, 1928.

Horton, George Moses. *Hope of Liberty*. Raleigh, NC: Joseph Gales and Son, 1829.
Poems By a Slave. Philadelphia. 1837.
Naked Genius. Raleigh, NC: Wm. Smith and Co., 1865.

Huff, William H. Sowing and Reaping.
From Deep Within. (n.d.)
I'm Glad I'm Who I Am. (n.d.)
Low Ground of Sorrow. (n.d.)

Hurston, Zora Neale. *Jonah's Gourd Vine.*
    Philadelphia: J.P. Lippincott, 1934.
    Their Eyes Were Watching God. 1937. rpt. New
    York: Negro Universities Press, 1969.
    Moses, Man of the Mountain. Philadelphia: J.B.
    Lippincott, 1939.
    Seraph on the Suwanee. New York: Charles
    Scribner's Sons, 1948.

Imbert, Dennis I. *The Colored Gentlemen.* 1931.
    rpt. New York: AMS Press, 1975.

Jamison, Roscoe Conkling. *Negro Soldiers and Other
    Poems.* Kansas City, KS: Press of Gray Printing
    Co., 1918.

Jenkins, Deadrick F. *It Was Not My World.* Los
    Angeles: Privately Printed, 1942.
    Letters to My Son. Los Angeles: The Deadrick F.
    Jenkins Publishing Co., 1947.

Johnson, Edward A. *Light Ahead for the Negro.* New
    York: Grafton Press, 1904.

Johnson, Georgia Douglas. *The Heart of a Woman, and
    Other Poems.* Boston: Cornhill, 1918.
    Bronze. Boston: B.J. Brimmer Co., 1922.
    Blue Blood. Appleton & Co., 1927.
    Plumes: a play in one act. New York: French,
    1927.
    Share My World. n.p.
    An Autumn Cycle. New York: Harold Vinal, LTD,
    1928.

Johnson, Helen Aurelia. *A First Harvest.* 1932.

Johnson, James Weldon. *The Autobiography of an Ex-
    Coloured Man.* 1912. rpt. New York: Knopf,
    1927.
    Fifty Years. Atlanta: Atlanta University Press,
    1913.
    Fifty Years and Other Poems. Boston: Cornhill,
    1917.
    God's Trombones. New York: Viking, 1927.
    *St. Peter Relates an Incident of the Resurrection
    Day.* New York: Viking Press, 1930.
    Selected Poems. n.p. 1936.

Johnson, Maggie Pogue. *Virginia Dreams.* Copyright by
    John Leonard, 1910.

Thoughts of Idle Hours. Roanoke, VA: Stone Printing and Mfg. Co., 1915.

Jones, Edward Smythe. *The Rose that Bloometh in My Heart and Other Poems*. Louisville, KY: 1908.
Souvenir Poem, Our Greater Louisville. Louisville, KY: 1908.
The Sylvan Cabin, a Centenary Ode on the Birth of Lincoln and Other Poems. Boston: Sherman French and Co., 1911.

Jones, Joshua Henry, Jr. *The Heart of the World and Other Poems*. Boston: Stratford Co., 1919.
Poems of the Four Seas. Boston: Cornhill, 1921.
By Sanction of Law. Boston: B.J. Brimmer Co., 1924.

Jones, J. McHenry. *Heart of Gold*. 1896. rpt. College Park, MD: McGrath, 1969.

Kinds, Levander. *Reflections*. Cleveland: Central Publishing House, 1946.

Killens, John Oliver. *Youngblood*. 1954. rpt. New York: Trident Press, Affiliate Publishers, 1966.

Laine, Henry Allen. *Footprints*. Richmond, KY: Cut Rate Publishing Co., 1914.

Lane, James Franklin. *My Second Trip Abroad*. (n.d.)
Much in Little. (n.d.)

Latimer, Lewis Howard. *Poems of Love and Life*. n.p.: Private, 1925.

Lee, George Washington. *River George*. New York: The McCauley Co., 1937.
Beale Street Sundown. New York: House of Field, 1942.

Lee, John Francis. *Poems*. Norfolk: Burke and Gregory Print, 1905.
What Ye Gon' Do Wif Ham. (n.d.)
Discords and Harmony. (n.d.)
The Prince and Ebony. (no imprint) 1907.

Love, Ruth Leary. *Nebraska and His Granny*. Tuskegee, AL: Tuskegee Institute Press, 1931.

Lyles, Aubrey. *Lazy Rhythm* (n.d.)
Darkydom. 1914, 1915.

   Running Wild. 1923.
   Rang Tang. 1927.
   Keep Shuffling. 1928.

Madgett, Naomi Long. *Songs to a Phantom Nightingale*.
   New York: Fortuny's Publishers, 1941.

Majors, Monroe Alpheus. *Ode to Frederick Douglass*.
   n.p. 1917.
   First Steps to Nursery Rhymes. n.p. 1921.

Mayfield, Julian. *Fire*. 1949.
   The Other Foot. 1952.
   World Full of Men. 1952.

Means, Sterling M. *The Black Devils and Other Poems*.
   Louisville, KY: Pentecostal Publishing, 1919.
   The Deserted Cabin and Other Poems. Atlanta:
   A.B. Caldwell Co., 1915.

Menard, John Willis. *Lays in Summer Lands*.
   Washington: Enterprise Publishing Co., 1879.

Miller, Clifford L. *Haunting Voice*. Lavalle, 1924.
   Wings Over Dark Waters: A Poetic Drama. New
   York: Great Concord Publishers, 1954.

Miller, Flournoy. *The Oyster Man*. 1907.
   Shuffle Along. 1921.
   Running Wild. 1923.
   Brownskin Models. 1927.
   Keep Shufflin'. 1928.
   Blackbirds. 1930.
   Lazy Rhythm. 1931.
   Meet Miss Jones. 1947.

Miller, May and Willis Richardson. *Negro History in
   Thirteen Plays*. Washington, D.C.: Associated.
   1923.

Mitchell, Loften. *The Cellar*. 1947.

Morrison, William Lorenzo. *Dark Rhapsody*. New York:
   H. Harrison, 1945.

Morse, Leonard Francis. *Dawn of Tomorrow*. Gulf City
   Printing Co., 1923.

Murphy, Beatrice. *Love Is a Terrible Thing*. New
   York: Hobson Book Press, 1945.

McBrown, Gertrude P. *The Picture Poetry Book*.
    Washington, D.C.: Associated, 1935.

McClellan, George Marion. *Poems and Storiettes*.
    Nashville: The Author, 1895.
    Songs of the South. Boston: Press of Rockwell
    and Churchill, 1896.
    Old Greenbottom Inn and Other Stories.
    Louisville, KY: The Author, 1906.
    The Path of Dreams. Louisville, KY: Morton,
    1916.

McGirt, James E. *Avenging the Maine*. Raleigh, NC:
    Edwards and Broughton Printers and Binders, 1899.
    *Some Simple Songs and a Few More Ambitious
    Attempts*. Philadelphia: George F. Lasher
    Printers and Binders, 1901.
    The Triumphs of Ephraim. Philadelphia: The
    McGirt Publishing Co., 1907.
    For Your Sweet Sake; Poems. Philadelphia: The
    John C. Winston Co., 1909.

Nash, Theodore E. D. *Love and Vengeance, or Viola's
    Victory*. Portsmouth, VA: Privately Printed,
    1903.

Nelson, Alice Ruth Moore Dunbar. *Violets and Other
    Tales*. Boston: Monthly Review Publishing, 1895.
    The Goodness of St. Roque and Other Stories.
    1899. rpt. College Park, MD: McGrath, 1969.

Newsome, Effie L. *Our Young People's Book of Verse*.
    Roberts and Sons, 1923.
    Gladiola Gardens. Washington, D.C.: Associated,
    1940.

Pawley, Thomas D., Jr. *Jedgement Day*. 1938.
    Smokey. 1938.
    Freedom in My Soul. 1938.
    Son of Liberty. 1938.

Payne, Daniel A. *Pleasures and Other Miscellaneous
    Poems*. Baltimore, MD: Sherwood and Co., 1850.

Pickens, William. *Bursting Bonds*. n.p.
    *The Vengeance of the Gods and Three Other Stories
    of the Real American Color Line Life*.
    Philadephia: AME Book Concern, 1922.
    American Aesop, Negro and Other Humor. Boston:
    Jordan and Moore Press, 1926.

Pitts, Richard. *Excelsior, Book of Poems.* Holly Springs, MS: Privately Printed, 1944.

Powell, Adam Clayton, Sr. *Picketing Hell.* New York: Wendell Publishing Malliett Co., 1942.

Ragland, J. Farley. *Lyrics and Laughter.* Lawrenceville, VA: The Brunswick Times Gazette Press, 1939.
The Hometown Sketchbook. Lawrenceville, VA: The Brunswick Times Gazette Press, 1940.
Rhymes of the Times. New York: W. Malliett and Co., 1946.

Razafenkeriefo, Andrea. *Hot Chocolates.* 1929.
Blackbirds. 1930.
Lazy Rhythm. 1931.

Redding, J. Saunders. *Stranger and Alone.* New York: Harcourt, Brace, 1950.

Richardson, Willis. *Plays and Pageants from the Life of the Negro.* Washington, D.C.: Associated, 1930.
Negro History in Thirteen Plays. Washington, D.C.: Associated, 1935.

Ridout, Daniel Lyman. *Verses from a Humble Cottage.* Hampton, VA: Hampton Institute Press, 1924.

Rogers, Alex. *In Dahomey.* 1902.
Abyssinia. 1906.
Bandanna Land. 1908.
Lode of Koal. 1909.
The Traitor. 1912.
Dark Town Follies. 1913.
The Old Man's Boy. 1914.
This and That. 1919.
Baby Blues. 1919.
Charlie. 1923.
Go-Go. 1923.
My Magnolia. 1926.

Rowe, George C. *Sunbeams.* Hampton: 1880.
Thoughts in Verse and a Volume of Poems. Charleston, SC: Kahrs, Stolze and Welch, 1887.
Our Heroes: Patriotic Poems on Men, Women, and Sayings of the Negro Race. Charleston, SC: Author, 1890.
Decoration. n.p. 1891.

Shackleford, Otis M. *Seeking the Best.* Kansas City, MO: Franklin Hudson Publishing Co., 1909.
Lillian Simmons. Kansas City, MO: Burton, 1915.

Shackleford, William H. *Pearls in Prose and Poetry.* Nashville: National Baptist Publishing Board, 1907.
Poems. Nashville, AMESSU Press, 1915.
Along the Highway. Nashville: AMESSU Press, 1916.

Shaw. O'Wendell. *Greater Need Below.* Columbus: Bi-Monthly Negro Book Club, 1936.

Shine, Ted. *Cold Day in August.* 1950.
Sho' Is Hot in the Cotton Patch. 1951.

Smith, Lucy. *No Middle Ground.* (n.p.)

Smith, S.P. *Our Alma Mater and Other Poems.* Washington, D.C.: Rev. A.C. Garner, 1904.

Stowers, Walter H. *Appointed.* 1894. rpt. New York: AMS Press, 1970.

Tarry, Ellen. *Janie Belle.* New York: Garden City Publishers, 1940.
Hezekiah Horton. New York: Viking Press, 1942.
My Dog Rinty. New York: Viking, 1946.
The Runaway Elephant. New York: Viking, 1950.

Thomas, David Gatewood. *The Voice from the Wilderness.* (n.d)

Tinsley, Tomi Carolyn, Lucia M. Pitts and Helen C. Harris. *Triad.* Washington, D.C.: Privately Printed, 1945.

Todd, Walter E. *Fireside Musings.* Washington, D.C.: Murray Brothers, 1909.
Gathered Treasures. Washington, D.C: Murray Bros., 1912.
A Little Sunshine. Washington, D.C.: Murray Bros., 1917.
Parson Johnson's Lecture. Washington, D.C.: Murray Bros., 1906.
Young Men's Christian Association (a poem). Washington, D.C.: Oscar D. Morris Printer, 1905.

Tolson, Melvin. *Rendezvous with America.* New York:

Dodd, Mead and Co., 1944.

Toomer, Jean. *Cane*. New York: Boni and Liverwright, 1923.

Tracy, Robert A. *The Sword of Nemesis*. New York: The Neal Publishing Co., 1919.

Turpin, Waters. *These Low Grounds*. New York: Harper, 1937.
O Canaan. New York: Doubleday, Doran, 1939.
The Rootless. New York: Vantage, 1957.

Tyler, Ephrain David. *Tyler's Poems*. Shreveport, LA: The Author (no imprint).

Walden, Islay. *Miscellaneous Poems*. Washington: Author, 1873.
Walden's Miscellaneous Poems, Which the Author Desires to Dedicate to the Cause of Education and Humanity. Washington, D.C.: Reid and Woodard Printers, 1872.
Walden's Sacred Poems, with a Sketch of His Life. New Brunswick, NJ: Terhune and Van Auglen's Press, 1877.

Walker, Margaret. *For My People*. New Haven: Yale University Press, 1942.

Walker, Thomas H. *Bebbly, or the Victorious Preacher*. Gainesville, FL: Pepper Publishing and Printing Co., 1910.
J. Johnson, or the Unknown Man; An Answer to Mr. Thomas Dixon's "Sins of the Fathers". Deland, FL: E.O. Painter Printing, 1915.

Waring, Robert Lewis. *As We See It*. Washington, D.C.: Press of C.F. Sudworth, 1910.

Waters, James C., Jr. *Shame of Duluth*. (n.d.)

Watkins, Lucian B. *Voices of Solitude*. Chicago: M.A. Donahue and Co., 1903.
The Old Rag Cabin. Russell, WY: The Printry, 1910.

Wheeler, Benjamin. *Cullings from Zion's Poets*. Mobile, AL: (no imprint) 1907.
The Varick Family. Mobile: n.p., 1907.

Wheeler, Charles Enoch. *Prelude* (a book of poems).

Privately Issued, 1943.

White, Walter. *Fire in the Flint*. 1924. rpt. New York: Negro Universities Press, 1969.
Flight. 1926. rpt. New York: Negro Universities Press, 1964.

Whitfield, Cupid A. *Poems of Today, or Some from the Everglades*. n.p.

Whitman, Albery A. *Leelah Misled*. Elizabethtown, KY: Richard LaRue, 1873.
Not a Man and Yet a Man. Springfield, OH: Republic Printing, 1877.
The Rape of Florida. St. Louis: Nixon-Jones Printing, 1884.
Twasinta's Seminoles; or The Rape of Florida. St. Louis: Nixon and Jones Printing Co., 1885.
The World's Fair Poems: The Freedman's Triumphant Song. Atlanta: Halsey, 1893.
An Idyll of the South. New York: Metaphysical Publishing Co., 1901.

Wilson, Harriet. *Our Nig: Or Sketches from the Life of a Free Black in a Two-Story White House, Showing that Slavery's Shadow Falls Over There, by "Our Nig"*. Boston: George C. Rand and Avery, 1859.
Our Nig. ed. Henry L. Gates, Jr. New York: Random House, 1983.

Wood, Charles Winter. *College Life*. (n.d.)
In Defense of Him. (n.d.)

Wood, John Wesley. *Lyrics of Sunshine*. Hord Brothers, 1922.

Wright, Richard. *Bright and Morning Star*. New York: International Publishers, 1938.
Uncle Tom's Children. New York: Harper and Bros., 1938.
Native Son. New York: Harper, 1940.
The Outsider. New York: Harper, 1953.

Wright, Julius C. *Poetic Diamonds*. Montgomery, AL: W.E. Allred Printing, 1906.

Yancey, Bessie Woodson. *Echoes from the Hills, a Book of Poems*. Washington, D.C.: Associated Printing, 1939.

Yerby, Frank. *Foxes of Harrow*. New York: Dial, 1946.

    The Vixens. New York: Dial, 1947.

    The Golden Hawk. New York: Dial, 1948.

    Pride's Castle. New York: Dial, 1949.

    Floodtide. New York: Dial, 1950.

    A Woman Called Fancy. New York: Dial, 1954.

    The Saracen Blade. New York: Dial, 1952.

    The Devil's Laughter. New York: Dial, 1953.

References

The following bibliography is a listing of those reference tools that proved most helpful in the compiling of the biobibliographical information included in this book. No attempt has been made to list the numerous texts, articles, or biographies that are available references for further information on some of the more noted writers. An asterisk precedes those volumes that were used as general reference tools; a number precedes those volumes that may prove helpful in further researching the writers included.

*   Abramson, Doris. *Negro Playwrights in the American Theatre, 1925-1959*. New York: Columbia University Press, 1969.

*   Adams, Russell L., ed. *Great Negroes Past and Present*. Chicago: Afro-American, 1969.

1   Adoff, Arnold. *The Poetry of Black America. Anthology of the Twentieth Century*. New York: Harper and Row, 1973.

*   *The American Negro Writer and His Roots: Selected Papers from the First Conference of Negro Writers*. New York: American Society of African Culture, 1960.

*   *Anglo-African Magazine*.

*   Arata, Esther Spring and Nichols, John R. *Black American Playwrights in the American Theatre, 1800 to the Present: A Bibliography*. Metuchen, NJ: The Scarecrow Press, Inc., 1976.

2   Bain, Robert, Flora, Joseph M., and Rubin, Louis D., Jr. *Southern Writers, a Biographical Dictionary*. Baton Rouge: Louisiana State University Press, 1979.

3   Baskin, Wade and Runes, Richard N. *Dictionary of Black Culture*. New York: Philosophical Library, 1973.

*   Belcher, Fannin S. "Negro Drama, Stage Center." *Opportunity* 17 (1939): 292-295.

*   Bennett, M.W. "Negro Poets." *Negro History Bulletin* 9 (1946): 171-172, 191.

4   Berlin, Ira, ed. *Freedom: A Documentary History of   Emancipation,   1861-1867.*   Cambridge: Cambridge University Press, 1983.

*   Bigsby, C.W.E., ed. *The Black American Writer.* Deland, FL: Everett Edwards, 1969.

5   Bond, Frederick W. *The Negro and the Drama.* 1940. rpt. College Park, MD: McGrath, 1969.

*   Bone, Robert A. *The Negro Novel in America.* New Haven: Yale University Press, 1966.

6   Bontemps, Arna. *Golden Slippers: An Anthology of Poetry for Young Readers.* New York: Harper and Row, 1941.

7   _____. *American Negro Poetry.* New York: Hill and Wang, 1963.

8   Bowden, Henry Warner. *Dictionary of American Religious   Biography.*   Westport,   CN: Greenwood Press, 1977.

*   Braithwaite, William Stanley. "The Negro in Literature." *Crisis* 28 (1924): 204-210.

*   _____. "Some Contemporary Poets of the Negro Race." *Crisis* 17 (1919): 275-280.

*   Brawley. Benjamin. *The Negro in Literature and Art.* New York: Doubleday, 1930.

*   Breman, Paul. *Sixes and Sevens.* London: Paul Breman, 1962.

*   Brignano, Russell C. *Black Americans in Autobiography, An Annotated Bibliography of Autobiographies   and Autobiographical Books Written Since the Civil War.* Durham: Duke University Press, 1974.

*   Brooks, Gwendolyn. "Poets Who Are Negro." *Phylon* 11 (1950): 312.

9   Brown, Charles A. and Dixon, John W., eds. *Stepping Stones.   A Compendium of Literary Efforts of Negroes in Birmingham, Alabama.* Birmingham: Southern University Press, 1961.

10 Brown, Sterling. *Negro Poetry and Drama*. Washington, D.C.: The Associates in Negro Folk Education, 1937.

11 _____, Davis, Arthur P., and Lee, Ulysses. *The Negro Caravan*. New York: Dryden, 1941.

12 Bucote, Samuel William. *Who's Who Among Colored Baptists*. Kansas City, MO: Franklin Hudson Publishing Co., 1913.

* Buscacca, Basil. "Checklist of Black Playwrights, 1823-1970." *Black Scholar* 5:1 (September 1973): 48-54.

* Byars, J.C., Jr. *Black and White*. 1927. rpt. Freeport, NY: Books for Libraries Press, 1971.

13 Calverton, V.F., ed. *An Anthology of American Negro Literature*. New York: The Modern Library, 1929.

* Campbell, Dorothy. *Index to Black American Writers in Collective Biographies*. Littleton, CO: Libraries Unlimited, Inc., 1983.

* *The Carolina Magazine.*

* Chandler, G. Lewis. "Coming of Age: A Note on American Novelists." *Phylon* 9 (1948): 25-29.

* Chapman, Abraham. *The Negro in American Literature and a Bibliography By and About Negro Americans*. Oshkosh, WI: Wisconsin Council of Teachers of English, 1966.

* Clark, Peter Wellington. *Arrows of Gold*. New Orleans: Xavier University Press, 1941.

14 Coleman, Edward Maceo, ed. *Creole Voices: Poems in French by Free Men of Color*. Washington, D.C.: Associated, 1945.

15 Cozart, Leland S. *A Venture of Faith. Barber-Scotia College, 1867-1967*. Heritage Printers, Inc., 1976.

* *The Crisis.*

16 Cromwell, Otelia, Turner, Lorenzo Dow and Dykes,
        Eva B., eds. *Readings from Negro Authors*.
        New York: Harcourt, Brace, 1931.

17 Cullen, Countee, ed. *Caroling Dusk: An Anthology
        of Verse by Negro Poets*. New York: Harper
        and Row, 1927.

18 Culp, Daniel Wallace, ed. *Twentieth Century Negro
        Literature*. *1902*. rpt. Miami: Mnemosyne
        Publishing Co., Inc., 1969.

19 Cunard, Nancy, ed. *Negro Anthology*. 1934. rpt.
        New York: Frederick UNgar, 1970.

20 Cuney, Waring, Hughes, Langston, and Wright,
        Bruce, eds. *Lincoln University Poets:
        Centennial Anthology*. New York: Fine
        Brothers, 1954.

21 Davenport, William Henry. *The Anthology of Zion
        Methodism*. Charlotte, NC: AME Zion
        Publishing House, 1925.

22 Davis, Arthur P. *From the Dark Tower: Afro-
        American Writers from 1900-1960*. Washington,
        D.C.: Howard University Press, 1974.

*   Davis, John P. *American Negro Reference Book*.
        Englewood Cliffs, NJ: Prentice-Hall, 1966.

23 Davis, Thadious M. and Harris, Trudier.
        *Dictionary of Literary Biography. Afro-
        American Fiction Writers After 1955*. Vol.
        33. Detroit: Gale Research Co., 1984.

*   Deodone, Frank and French, William P. Black
        *American Poetry Since 1944: A Preliminary
        Checklist*. Chatham, NJ: Chatham, 1971.

24 Dreer, Herman. *American Literature by Negro
        Authors*. New York: MacMillan, 1950.

*   Edmonds, Randolph. "Black Drama in the American
        Theatre: 1700-1970." In *The American
        Theatre: A Sum of Its Parts*. New York:
        Samuel French, 1971: 397-426.

*   Eleazer, Robert B. *Singers in the Dawn*.
        Atlanta: Conference on Education and Race
        Relations, 1934.

* Emanuel, James. *Dark Symphony. Negro Literature in America.* New York: Free Press, 1968.

25 Evans, Mari. *Black Women Writers (1950-1980).* Garden City, NY: Doubleday, 1983.

* *Fire!! Devoted to Younger Artists.* 1926. rpt. Westport: Negro Universities Press, 1970.

* Ford, Nick Aaron. *Black Insights: Significant Literature by Black Americans, 1760 to the Present.* Waltham, MA: Ginn, 1971.

* _____ and Faggett, H.L., eds. *Best Short Stories by Afro-American Writers, 1924-1950.* Boston: Mendor, 1950.

* French, William P., Fabre, Micheal J., and Singh, Amiritjit. *Afro-American Poetry and Drama, 1760-1975.* Detroit: Gale Research Co., 1979.

* Gale, Zona. "The Negro Sees Himself." *Survey* 54 (1925): 300-301.

* Gayle, Addison. *The Way of the New World: The Black Novel in America.* Garden City, NJ: Doubleday, 1975.

* Green, Elizabeth Atkinson Lay. *The Negro in Contemporary American Literature.* College Park, MD: McGrath, 1928.

* Gubert, Betty Kaplan. *Early Black Bibliographies.* 1863-1918. New York: Garland Publishing, Inc., 1982.

* Hatch, James V. "A White Folks Guide to 200 Years of Black and White Drama." *The Drama Review* 16: 4 (1972): 5-24.

* _____ and Omani Abdullah. *Black Playwrights, 1823-1977: An Annotated Bibliography.* New York: R.R. Rowker, 1977.

* _____ and Ted Shine, eds. *Black Theatre, USA: 1847-1974.* New York: Harcourt, Brace and World, 1976.

* Hayden, Robert. *Kaleidoscope.* New York: Harcourt, Brace and World, 1967.

*   Herman, Kali. *Women in Particular. An Index to America.* Phoenix, AZ: The Orynx Press, 1984.

26 Hill Herbert, ed. *Anger and Beyond: The Negro Writer in the United States.* New York: Harper and Row, 1966.

27 _____. *Soon One Morning: New Writing by American Negroes, 1940-1962.* New York: Knopf, 1968.

*   Hughes, Carl M. *The Negro Novelist, 1940-1950.* New York: Citadel Press, 1953.

28 Hughes, Langston and Bontemps. *The Poetry of the Negro, 1746-1970.* Garden City, New York: Doubleday, 1970.

*   Hughes, Langston. *New Negro Poets, U.S.A.* Bloomington: Indiana University, 1964.

29 Ikonne, Chidi. *From DuBois to Van Vechten: The Early New Negro Literature, 1903-1926.* Westport: The Greenwood Press, 1981.

*   Inge, M. Thomas, Duke, Maurice, and Bryer, Jackson R. *Black American Writers.* New York: St. Martin's Press, 1978.

*   Jackson, Augusta Victoria. "The Renascence of Negro Literature, 1922-1929." Atlanta University, Georgia, 1936 (Thesis).

30 Jackson, Blyden and Rubin, Louis D., Jr. *Black Poetry in America.* Baton Rouge: Louisiana State University Press, 1974.

31 Johnson, Charles Spurgeon. *Ebony and Topaz, a Collection.* New York: Opportunity, National Urban League, 1927.

32 Johnson, James Weldon, ed. *The Book of American Negro Poetry.* New York: Harcourt Brace, 1931.

33 Johnson, Abby Arthur and Johnson, Ronald Maberry. *Propaganda and Aesthetics.* Amherst: The University of Massachusetts Press, 1979.

*   Kerlin, Robert T. *Contemporary Poetry of the Negro*. Hampton, VA: Hampton Institute Press, 1923.

*   Littlejohn, David. *Black on White: A Critical Survey of Writing by American Negroes*. New York: Grossman, 1966.

*   Lanusse, Armand. *Creole Voices: Poems in French by Free Men of Color*. Washington D.C.: Associated Publishers, 1845.

35   Lloyd, James A., ed. *Lives of Mississippi Authors, 1817-1967*. Jackson: University of Mississippi Press, 1981.

*   Locke, Alain Leroy. *The New Negro*. New York: Boni and Liveright, 1925.

36   Logan, Rayford W. and Winston, Micheal R. *Dictionary of American Negro Biography*. New York: W.W. Norton, 1982.

*   Loggins, Vernon. *The Negro Author, His Development in America to 1900*. New York: Columbia University Press, 1931.

*   Long, Richard A. *A Select Chronology of Afro-American Prose and Poetry, 1760-1970*. CAAS Bibliography No. 9. Atlanta: Center for African and African American Studies.

37   Mapp, Edward. *Directory of Blacks in the Performing Arts*. Metuchen, NJ: The Scarecrow Press, Inc., 1978.

*   Margolies, Edward and Bakish, David. *Afro-American Fiction, 1853-1976*. Detroit: Gale Research Co., 1979.

*   Matthews, Geraldine O. and the African American Materials Project Staff of the School of Library Services, North Carolina Central University, Durham, North Carolina. *Black American Writers, 1773-1949: A Bibliography and Union List*. Boston: G.K. Hall and Co., 1975.

*   *The Messenger*.

*   Miller, Ruth. *Black American Literature: 1760-
       Present*. Beverly Hills, CA: Glencoe Press,
       1971.

*   Morton, Lena Beatrice. *Negro Poetry in America*.
       Boston: Stratford, 1925.

38 Murphy, Beatrice M. *Ebony Rhythm*. 1948. rpt.
       Freeport, NY: Books for Libraries Press,
       1968.

*   *The Negro Almanac.*

39 _____. *Negro Voices*. New York: Harrison, 1938.

*   *The Negro Handbook: An Annual Encyclopedia of the
       Negro*.   Tuskegee   Institute, Alabama, 1912-
       1967.

*   *Negro History Bulletin.*

40 Neyland, Leedell and Riley, John W.   *The History
       of Florida Agricultural and Mechanical
       University*.   Gainesville: University of
       Florida Press, 1963.

41 O'Brien, John.   *Interviews With Black Writers*.
       New York: Liveright, 1973.

*   *Opportunity.*

*   Ovington, Mary White. *Portraits in Color*. New
       York: Viking Press, 1927.

*   Oxley, Thomas L.G.   "Survey of Negro Literature,
       1760-1926."   *The   Messenger* 9 (February
       1927): 37-39.

42 Page, James A. and Jae Min Roh. *Selected Black
       American   and   Carribbean   Authors,   a
       Biobibliography*.   Littleton, CO: Libraries
       Unlimited, 1985.

*   Parker, John W.   "The Emergence of Negro
       Fiction."   *Negro History Bulletin* 12 (1948):
       12, 18.

*   Patterson, Lindsay, ed. *Anthology of the American
       Negro in the Theatre*. Washington D.C.:
       Association for the Study of Negro Life and
       History, 1967.

*   Pawley, Thomas.   "The First Black Playwrights."
        Black World 21 (April 1972):   16, 24.

43   Perkins, A.E.   *Who's Who in Colored Louisiana*.
        Baton Rouge: Douglas Loan Co., Inc., 1930.

*   Ploski, Harry A. and Kaiser, Ernest.   *The Negro
        Almanac*. New York: Bellwether, 1971.

*   _____, Lindenmayer, Otto J., and Kaiser, Ernest,
        eds.   *Reference   Library   of   Black   America*.
        Chicago: Afro-American Press, 1971.

44   Pool, Rosey E.   *Beyond the Blues*.   England: The
        Hand and FLower Press, 1962.

*   Porter,   Dorothy B.   *North American Negro Poets: A
        Bibliographic   Checklist   of   Their   Writings,
        1760-1944*.   Hattiesburg, MS: The Book Farm,
        1945.

*   Randall,   Dudley,   ed.   *The Black Poets*.   New York:
        Bantam Books, 1981.

*   Redding, Saunders.   "The Negro Author: His
        Publisher,   His   Public   and   His   Purse."
        Publishers Weekly, (1945):   1284-1288.

45   Richmond, Phillis.   *Bid the Vassal Soar*.
        Washington,   D.C.:   Howard   University   Press,
        1975.

46   Robinson,   William   N.   *Early Black American Poets*.
        Dubuque, Iowa: Wm. C. Brown, 1969.

47   Rollins, Charlemae Hill.   *They Showed the Way*.
        New York: Crowell, 1964.

48   Rousseve, Charles Barthelmy.   *The Negro in
        Louisiana*.   New   Orleans: Xavier University
        Press, 1927.

49   Rush, Theresa Gunnels, Myers, Carol Fairbanks
        and   Arata,   Esther   Spring.   *Black   American
        Writers,   Past   and   Present*.   Metuchen,   NJ:
        Scarecrow Press, 1975.

50   Scally, Mary Anthony.   *Negro Catholic Writers,
        1900-1943*.   Detroit: W.   Roming   and   Co.,
        1945.

*   Schomberg, Arthur A. *A Bibliographical Checklist
     of American Negro Poetry*. New York: Charles
     F. Heartman, 1916.

51 The Scribes. *Sing, Laugh, Weep: A Book of Poems
     by the Scribes*. St. Louis: Scribes Press,
     1944.

52 Sherman, Joan R. *Invisible Poets*. Urbana:
     University of Illinois Press, 1974.

*   Shockley, Ann A. and Chandler, Sue. *Living Black
     American   Authors: A   Biographical
     Dictionary*. New York: Bowker, 1973.

53 Simmons, William J. *Men of Mark: Eminent,
     Progressive and Rising*. Cleveland: George
     M. Rewell and Co., 1887.

*   Stetson, Erlene. *Black Sister: Poetry by Black
     American Women*. Indiana University Press,
     1981.

*   Thurman, Wallace. "Negro Poets and Their
     Poetry." *Bookman* 67 (1928): 555-561.

54 Troup, C.V. *Distinguished Negro Georgians*.
     Dallas: Royal Publishing Co., 1962.

*   Turner, Darwin T. "The Negro Novelist in the
     South."   *Southern   Humanities   Review*   I
     (1967): 21-29.

*   _____. *Black Drama in America: An Anthology*.
     Greenwich: Fawcett, 1971.

*   _____. *Afro-American Writers*. Northbrook, IL:
     AHM Publishing Corporation, 1970.

*   Waldrop, Ruth W. *Alabama Authors: Books in
     Print*.   Huntsville,   AL: The   Strode
     Publishers, Inc., 1980.

*   Wade-Gayles, Gloria Jean. *No Crystal Stair:
     Visions of Race and Sex in Black Women's
     Fiction*. New York: Pilgrim Press, 1984.

55 Wagner, Jean. *Black Poets of the United States:
     from Paul Laurence Dunbar to Langston
     Hughes*. Chicago: University of Illinois
     Press, 1973.

*   Walker, Margaret. "New Poets." *Phylon* 11
        (1950): 345-354.

56   White, Newman I. and Jackson, Walter C.   *An
        Anthology   of   Verse   by   American   Negroes*.
        Durham, NC: Moore Publishing Co., 1968.

*   Whiteman, Maxwell. *A Century of Fiction by
        American   Negroes,   1853-1952.   A Descriptive
        Bibliography*. Philadephia: Press of Maurice
        Jacobs, 1955.

*   Whitlow, Roger. *Black American Literature, a
        Critical   History*.   Totowa, NJ: Littlefield,
        Adams, & Co., 1974.

57   *Who's Who in Colored America, 1930-1932*.

*   Williams, Ethel L. *Biographical Directory of
        Negro Ministers*. New York: Scarecrow, 1965.

*   Work, Monroe, ed. *The Negro Yearbook, An Annual
        Encyclopedia   of   the Negro*. Tuskegee: Negro
        Yearbook Publishing Co., 1925.

58   Wright, Richard R., Jr. *Centennial Encyclopedia
        of   the   AME   Church*.   Philadephia: Book
        Concern of the AME Church, 1916.

59   Yellin, Jean Fagan. *The Intricate Knot: The
        Negro   in American Literature, 1776-1863*. New
        York: University Press, 1971.

*   Young, James. *Black Writers of the Thirties*.
        Baton   Rouge: Louisiana   State   University
        Press, 1973.

About the Compiler

M. MARIE BOOTH FOSTER is Assistant Professor of Languages and Literature at Florida A&M University.

www.ingramcontent.com/pod-product-compliance
Lightning Source LLC
Chambersburg PA
CBHW060348100426
42812CB00003B/1173